MAR 2 2 2018

NO LONGER PROPERTY OF
SEATTLE PUBLIC LIBRARY

2017

The Best Women's
Stage Monologues

D0730924

MAR 3 8 2018

2017
THE BEST WOMEN'S
STAGE MONOLOGUES

Edited and with a Foreword

by Lawrence Harbison

MONOLOGUE AUDITION SERIES

SMITH AND KRAUS PUBLISHERS   2017

© 2017 by Smith and Kraus Publishers, Inc., *2017 The Best Women's Stage Monologues* is fully protected under the copyright laws of the United States of America and of all countries covered by the International Copyright Union (including the Dominion of Canada and the rest of the British Commonwealth), The Berne Convention, the Pan-American Copyright Convention and the Universal Copyright Convention as well as all countries with which the United States has reciprocal copyright relations. All rights, including professional/amateur stage rights, motion picture, recitation, lecturing, public reading, radio broadcasting, television, video or sound recording, all other forms of mechanical or electronic reproduction, such as CD-ROM, CD-I, DVD, information storage and retrieval systems and photocopying, and the rights of translation into foreign languages, are strictly reserved.

All rights reserved.

ISBN: 9781575259130
Library of Congress Control Number: 2329-2709

Typesetting and layout by Elizabeth E. Monteleone
Cover by Olivia Monteleone

A Smith and Kraus book
177 Lyme Road, Hanover, NH 03755
editorial 603.643.6431 To Order 1.877.668.8680
www.smithandkraus.com

TABLE OF CONTENTS

Here you will find a rich and varied selection of monologues for women from plays most of which were produced and/or published in the 2016-2017 theatrical season. Many are for younger performers (teens through thirties) but there are also some excellent pieces for older women as well. Some are comic (laughs), some are dramatic (generally, no laughs). Some are rather short, some are rather long. All represent the best in contemporary playwriting.

Several of the monologues are by playwrights whose work may be familiar to you, such as Don Nigro, Steven Dietz, Sheila Callaghan, Aaron Posner, Stephen Belber, Lee Blessing and Theresa Rebeck; others are by exciting up-and-comers such as Nicole Pandolfo, Graham Techler, Gregory Strasser, Jacqueline Goldfinger, Kim Davies, C.S. Hanson and Carey Crim.

Many of the plays from which these monologues have been culled have been published and, hence, are readily available either from the publisher/licensor or from a theatrical book store such as the Drama Book Shop in New York. A few plays may not be published for a while, in which case contact the author or his agent to request a copy of the entire text of the play which contains the monologue which suits your fancy. Information on publishers/rights holders may be found in the Rights & Permissions section in the back of this anthology.

> NOTE: the monologue copy indicates age, race and sex of the character as originally conceived by the playwright. Many monologues could be used in class or for auditions by any age, race or sex.

Break a leg in that audition! Knock 'em dead in class!

Lawrence Harbison

The Monologues

ALIVE AND WELL

Kenny Finkle

Dramatic
Carla Keenan, thirties

Carla has been hired to write a story for a magazine about a Confederate ghost known as the "Lonesome Soldier." She has enlisted the help of a Civil War reenactor named Zach, to whom she is speaking.

CARLA

Queechee Vermont. Have you ever heard of it Mr. Clemenson? My grandmother had a house there. When I was little we'd go up there for the summer. And my grandmother had a fireplace. And on cool summer nights she'd light it. The first time I sat in front of her fireplace I was afraid. I didn't want to get too close so she took out some marshmallows and we made smores. That got me closer to the fire. The smores. S'mores. Smores. I want some smores right now. Wouldn't it be great if we had smores? When I was eight I ate marshmallows for seven days straight once. I love marshmallows. Marshmallows, marshmallows, marshmallows, mersh-mallllsss … My grandmother loved marshmallows too. She taught me about art. My grandmother did. She used to take me to museums every Saturday when I was growing up and we'd look at art together. And she was an artist too. She wouldn't have called herself that though, she would have called herself a housewife. But she did make art, Mr. Clemenson. Beautiful art. She had this one piece, I don't know how to explain it, it's just a piece of marble that she shaped in two concentric pieces but one of the sides comes to a point, and out of it there's a break in the marble, a different color, a red, that makes a line down to the bottom of the piece, a little crack of red in the grey. And it makes me feel so much pain. And I don't know why. I want to know why it makes me feel. She just died. She was the most important person in my life. I'd talk to her about everything and now I have no one to talk to about anything. I'm lost without her. I don't know who I am or what I'm supposed to be doing anymore. I don't know right from wrong. I've lost my moral compass. I've lost my way.

ALIVE AND WELL

Kenny Finkle

Seriocomic
Carla, thirties

Carla has been hired to write a story for a magazine about a Confederate ghost known as the "Lonesome Soldier." She has enlisted the help of a Civil War reenactor named Zach, to whom she is speaking.

CARLA

My fiance'. Ex fiancé. He just left me. Screw you Lou! I hate Lou. That's not true. Lou says I have a compulsive need to tell the truth all the time. He says when I lie, even the littlest lie it seems to haunt me, like the telltale heart and then I have to confess. And it's true I do, and Mr. Clemenson, I've been haunted for days now because I have a lot to confess to you. Mr. Clemenson, I'm here under somewhat false pretenses ... I don't know who I'm working for ... I got this job from an ad on Craigslist! I took the job for the money. Five thousand dollars! That's how much I'm getting paid! The ad said they were a major magazine and they sent me half my fee and I'm supposed to get the rest when I turn in the story and 2500 dollars is a lot of money for me right now because I can't pay my rent because Lou left me and my credit cards are maxed and I used to write for a newspaper but newspapers are dying and so I was fired and I can't seem to get another job and I've won awards! But no one cares. That's not true, people care but not enough people so I was cut. And that made me angry. That's not true, I was angry before that. That's not true, I wasn't angry, I was misunderstood and that makes me angry because no one understands me. Not even Lou. When we were at the Virginia Diner that was him that texted me. He was in the apartment getting his stuff and he wanted to know who should get the Joni Mitchell cds. "I get the Joni Mitchell cds dillweed I get them!!" Which is what I texted him. He should have known that! Why didn't he know that? He should have known that I love Joni Mitchell! Joni Mitchell tells the truth! Joni Mitchell is my idol! I wish I were Joni Mitchell singing the truth at the top of my lungs

THE ARSONISTS

Jacqueline Goldfinger

Dramatic
M, twenties

M and H were a father-daughter arson team. A fire they set went awry, he died, but she is holding onto his ghost. M is speaking to her father's ghost about her mother's death. She is trying to express to him why she just can't let him go.

M

The night before her funeral. You ripping out yourself in the woods. I sneaked over to the funeral home. Crawled into the coffin. I crawled in, all eight years squished between the smooth velvet and her cold arm. And I reached up to hold her face. To give her a kiss and say I love you and I'm sorry and if I did this, if I did, if this was my fault, I'm sorry, it was probably my fault. It was probably my, because I was a—let's be truth now—I was a pain in the ass. And I's so sorry. And to come on back home. I'll be good. But when I reached up to hold, to kiss, I couldn't get to her face. I couldn't because there wasn't no face there. There wasn't, There was a chin, And a mouth, And a nose, And bandages. And I couldn't reach, or untie or unfold, or fold with or to or between us, I couldn't. I tried. I did. I'm sorry, Momma, I'm trying but I can't reach you. And so I gave her a kiss on the cheek And snuggled down underneath her arm. And the next morning The burial man find me And he says, "You can't be here young lady. You a bad young lady. Bad girl. Bad." And he shoved me off. But in that long last night, I held her. I held her and I knew it was just gonna be me and you, Daddy. Me and you, forever. No one else. No one else to cry or scream or … Any of us. Just us. And now there are pieces missing from both of you. And I don't want to find 'em. Because it only means you'll go away.

For information on this author, click on the WRITERS tab att
www.smithandkraus.com.

BED

Sheila Callaghan

Dramatic
Holly, twenties

Holly is speaking to her newborn daughter.

HOLLY

my teacup
my shucked oyster
my carbomb
your mouse-cries sift over me like dry rice
you have two souls
one is mild and fine-spun
the other arrogant and histrionic
I can't tell which is closer to the truth
But I suppose that's not for me to judge
I have two things to tell you
One is a secret
And the other is a prayer.
Here is the secret:
Loving you has made me scandalously beautiful
Did you know when we're apart
the phantom limb of you spasms in me?
How long will that last?

    Beat.

Sometimes
I think of you as a grown woman
robust and autonomous
hiking through the snow at night
on your way back from the bars
Your boozy breath in clouds against the night
your cheeks raw from wind and whisky
he's waiting for you back home
He made you coffee
half milk, frothy, in a huge ceramic mug
you whack the snow from your boots

you sit down to the table
and as you raise the hot mug to your lips
you think of a hay ride
A bent hubcap
the color of twilight
cartwheels in a clean patch of grass
stories plowed from the field of your own history
And he watches you drink
And he loves you rigidly, with intention
And I'm so so fucking grateful you get to have this
You get to have everything
So
eat the world, girly
crush it between your molars
suck those rivers dry
and give me the strength to give you the strength
to amplify
forever

BIG SKY

Alexandra Gersten-Vassilaros

Comic
Tessa, seventeen

Tessa is all dressed up and about to go out with the Boss's daughter, which is not something she's looking forward to. Jonathan, who is like an uncle to her, reluctantly shares a joint with Tessa. Her cozy relationship with Jonathan, combined with a few hits of weed make it impossible for her to keep a secret. Her brand new love for Catoni, who is completely out of her frame of reference, is waking her up in every way possible.

TESSA

His name is Catoni. He's half Native American, quarter Dominican, quarter Haitian and wicked gorgeous. And he's so amazing and deep - the grandson of a chief. A fucking chief! I'm totally obsessed with his penis—which is attached to a beautiful body which is attached to a beautiful head within which there lies a beautiful expansive mind. The porter job in our building is only part-time. His long-term plan is to save enough money to open an alcohol and drug rehab in Shinnecock. He lives on the reservation there and belongs to an actual _tribe_. In the Hamptons! He wants to fight the fight for reparations, a return of territories, he goes to conferences … Seriously, there's this big argument among the tribe on whether or not they should open a casino on the rez and, of course, he's like totally against it because he says it's all part of the endless alienation of his people's true nature, enshrining money, lust and dis-humanity. Like, is that not the coolest word ever!! Dis-humanity! He says that we're all living under a skewed social order that operates under a turbo-powered capitalistic paradigm, seriously dedicated to the enrichment and fortification of the white man, who he believes is basically a parasitic mutation feeding off the planet, blindly dedicated to its own demise. He says that the real purpose of being born is to align ourselves to the divine forces informing the world around us and within us. He says that we've lost the plot of what it means to be human. And, oh my god, his body - I swear, Jonathan, just looking at him makes me feel so—happy, deeply happy which is progress you know, cuz I go through these seriously fucked up phases of hating close contact because it's just so awkward and scary. But Catoni says awkward is real and real is sexy, and wh.. he talks like that everything just, just falls away … like all my *clothes* for instance.

For information on this author, click on the WRITERS tab at www.smithandkraus.com.

BIG SKY
Alexandra Gersten-Vassilaros

Dramatic
Jen, mid to late forties

The family is stuck in a luxury condo in a daunting snow storm and her daughter has just had a car accident. The lights are out, there is no food or electricity and tension is high between everyone. Jen can barely absorb the things her husband and daughter have just said to her, all of which seemed cruel, though possibly true. Enraged and frightened, she has just told her husband she wants to leave him. As soon as she's said it, she feels she must explain and defend herself to Tessa and Jack. Everything is on the line for her. The truth of what she's been going through pours out, unfiltered.

JEN

Do not forget that I was a highly responsible, highly highly functioning devoted woman mother and wife for nearly half my life, on everyone's team every step of the way and I have done everything in my power to to pull myself together but between the unexpected arrival of menopause, which, by the way, should *never ever* be referred to as *THE* menopause because that sounds, that sounds like some sort of joke instead of the highly complicated biological transformational trial by fire that it is - growing is required … but will someone tell me how to do that? My mother's illness and death 3 years ago, your father's slide into Alzheimer's, our best friends getting divorced or or diagnosed with cancer, your job loss and virtual disappearance, depression, which I looked up, online, depression, a serious medical condition in which a person feels unimportant, sad or hopeless, slumping in the den for 18 months, and I tried to be a good wife, the optimistic blah blah "loving" wife to the rescue but there's only so much a person can do to rescue another person, if it's even possible, except except Pederson seemed to do it so much better and faster, so about face everybody, get on board—the gravy train is back on track speeding thru all the stations again and now, and now, our only child is going to leave *home,* the the organizing principle, Tessa, the light of our life is walking, skipping out the door which means that it's just gonna be you and me, you and me roasting marshmallows with clumps of white men and their handbag wives talking about the TV shows they stream before bed. I hate that the word "streaming" has nothing whatsoever to do with water. I hate that! My god, I don't think I have whatever it is a middle-aged woman needs to make it through to the other side. The other side of what? I can't, I can't seem to make any good part of me come back to life. So if I seem lost ... it's because I am. LOST. You're right Tessa, I am a mess. And then one day I try to get things in per.. perspective. Shake myself off, try to be ... useful. And I meet this man, this fragile honest man, simple—and I start, I start there, right there, no past, no future, just this teeny tiny moment with someone who actually likes eye contact and listens ... and makes me feel less alone."

For information on this author, click on the WRITERS tab at
www.smithandkraus.com.

THE BELLE OF BELMAR
Nicole Pandolfo

Comic
Lorna, thirty-five

Lorna, a single mom, is registering on a dating website.

LORNA

Name: Lorna L. Age: 35. Mid thirties- no, EARLY thirties … Location: Jersey Girl (Belmar)! Looking for: Long-term dating. Likes: My daughter, the beach, shopping, looking at the stars, going out in The City, Scandal (the TV show), country music especially the Dixie Chicks, built guys, aerosol hair spray, red nail polish, Grey Goose, any and all kinds of pasta. Dislikes: Fake people, winter, married men. About me: I work in the office for the county as a receptionist. Now that my daughter will be going to college in the fall I am considering going to school too. My friends all tell me I'm a lot of fun to hang out with and that I am very smart. I never forget to shave and I make really good cocktails and spaghetti Bolognese. I'm learning how to bake, and am not afraid to get dirty (in the kitchen of course)! I'm a Gemini. If you are a Leo or a Sagittarius we'd probably really get along, but if you're a Taurus we might need to work a little harder at it, but I'm up for a challenge! My idea of a perfect night is a sunset walk on the beach followed by happy hour with classy hors d'oeuvres on my front steps and then a nice Omaha steak cooked on the grill with some pasta salad and a few vegetables to be healthy (p.s. I know how to make this meal). Then we'd snuggle on my couch and watch something on Netflix or HBO if you have an account. I also really love to go out so we could substitute cooking in for a night on the town in The City or even here in Belmar. I know which places have the best clams on the half shell. If we hit it off I can share this top-secret knowledge with you). Also, since I am an easy-going person I am up for almost anything, especially being whisked away to Paris or Sandals, Jamaica. As you see I am only interested in long-term dating. Please do not message me if you are just looking to hook-up because I am not interested. Seriously. And if you are STILL MARRIED AND NOT SEPARATED PLEASE DO NOT MESSAGE ME. THAT MEANS YOU EDWIN MACERO. STOP MESSAGING ME

FROM DIFFERENT ACCOUNTS OR I'M GONNA CALL MY COUSIN TINO WHO IS AN EX-MARINE.

For information on this author, click on the WRITERS tab at www.smithandkraus.com.

THE BELLE OF BELMAR

Nicole Pandolfo

Comic
Lorna, thirty-five

Lorna, a single mom who is something of a shopaholic, calls a psychic hotline for shopping and then dating advice.

LORNA

Psychic Hotline? I'm calling because I have a few questions for you. Ok. Yes. Ok. Great. One of the things I'm wondering about is whether or not to buy this Kate Spade mini-satchel in burnt tangerine that would go really great with understated neutrals and that I believe could carry me from autumn to winter and even into spring and summer with the right accessories. It's on final sale for $235 which is a significant discount, but of course it cannot be returned and the last time I tried to sell something on Ebay I ended up having to pay the buyer ... it's a long story ... Oh my God. Ok. Yes. I mean it works with all four seasons. I mean it's an investment, but you know, you gotta invest in yourself right? ... I so agree. Ok. Great. My next question. There is this guy who messaged me on Match who apparently went to my high school, but of course I don't remember him, but he seems really nice and cute and it looks like he has an actual job and is divorced for three years now and has one daughter who is 9 which I think is a great age and his wife is remarried so she shouldn't be too much trouble, but I've really never been into blondes, but he's sort of a strawberry-blonde which is really cute, he's Irish I think, which is like, hey—Luck o' the Irish, am I right. But I'm just not sure what to do about him because normally I don't date people who remember me from high school, but I'm wondering if there is any indication on your end whether or not I should say yes or ... Ok. Ok. I see. How long should I wait to reply? ... Ok, normally I reply two weeks later ... You really think that's too long? Well once I replied right away and the guy thought I was an escort and ... Ok got it. Great. I'll message him tomorrow afternoon. One last question. My daughter. Denise. She wants to go away to college in Boston, but see, she's had a rough year and I think that's too far and that I should tell her no. Are you getting a reading one way or another on this, because this is pretty urgent and I'm hoping for some cosmic revelations. I'm getting another call. Can you hold? Wait, how much is that a minute? … Maybe I'd better call you back. Ah- it's beeping again. Gotta go.

For information on this author, click on the WRITERS tab at www.smithandkraus.com.

BIG CITY

Barbara Blumenthal-Ehrlich

Seriocomic
Sandy, twenties-thirties

Sandy is an eccentric stranger who Joe picked up in line for Chinese takeout. He's just come through the door with Sandy, and she's describing his impassioned—and very public—plea for connection. Sandy speaks to Joe's puzzled roommate, Jane, who sometimes sleeps with him.

SANDY

You said we had something special. Something he's been searching for all his life. Humanity. I've been searching for it all my life too. But I'd given up. If you knew … If I told you about the men in my life. The inhumanity of love. Not just love, the world. I walk around the city, head down, staring at my feet. Willing them to move. Surrendering myself, totally and completely, to the sidewalk. But he forced me to look up. He grabbed me. I mean, in a physical way. He squeezed me by both arms 'till it hurt and said, "You're all that separates me from the great abyss. You are the very embodiment of humanity. You are a human being." And then he looked deep into my eyes, deeper than anyone's ever looked before, and he said, "Do you know what I mean?" And I said I did. Because I did. And he wept. Right there in Chow Down's. Good, clean tears that could wash away the mess of anything, anywhere. Windex tears. Formula 409 tears. Tears like I never saw before. Each one a pearl. Everyone in the place stared at him. Not to make a spectacle out of him or anything, but because they knew what he meant too. They were nodding and smiling. At that moment I realized, My God, I'm not alone.

For information on this author, click on the WRITERS tab at
www.smithandkraus.com.

BIRDS OF A FEATHER

June Guralnick

Comic
Diana, twenties

Diana Katherine Birdwhistle is an early 20th Century New York fashionista magazine columnist for Harper's, with a rapier wit and razor-sharp intellect. Harper's has limited her articles to gossip about the fashionable set and their latest conquests and chapeaus. Here, Diana dances around sticking pins in a voodoo kewpie doll.

DIANE

Who saw her die?
I, said the fly.
Kewpie doll, kewpie doll
Time for you to cry.

(She stops dancing, holds up doll, and imitates her editor.).

Why, why did I expect more from a woman editor and suffragist to boot?

(imitating her editor)

"Your devotion to our avian friends is admirable, but your descriptive—some might even say gruesome—account of the feather trade: "Bird Guts On Our Hats, Blood on Our Hands," is best left for a different type of publication. This is not the type of article our discerning readers expect of society's favorite daughter, Diana Katherine Birdwhistle, acclaimed authoress of "Fashions Moderne of the Civilized World and Beyond." We must give our readers what they desire from you—fashion advice with a soupçon of superiority and good taste!

(She chants and sticks more pins into the doll.)

Les femmes are worse than men when it comes to giving a gal a break. My departure from Harper's this morning was *très amusant.* "My dear, dear Miss Jordan, I am so terribly sorry. The Tiffany lamp mysteriously leapt into my hands and then, mon Dieu—I was as much surprised as you—magically flew up, up, up, , crashing into that *magnifique* crystal ball chandelier!"

(She throws doll into the fireplace.)

Here's something to warm your icy heart! Glass balls—and glass ceilings—need to be broken! The world hasn't seen the end of reporter Kate Bird yet. Other publications will be eager to print my feather exposé. Goodbye, Diana Birdwhistle, Queen of the Fashionable Set. Hello, Kate Bird, Princess of the Plumed World. Birds of a feather must flock together.

BIRDS OF A FEATHER

June Guralnik

Comic
Lady Birdwhistle, fifties

BIRDS OF A FEATHER takes place in 1912. Lady Birdwhistle's daughter, Diana, has introduced a number of modern appliances into the Birdwhistle residence. The treadmill is the last straw for Lady Birdwhistle. Disheveled from a recent run-in with a street sweeping machine, she has recently returned to the safety of her home.

LADY BIRDWHISTLE

Oh dear, oh dear, oh dear! As we stoutly, stalwartly and seditiously departed the National Women's Suffrage meeting, at which Lady Birdwhistle was elected Undersecretary to the Secretary, two gargantuan, glowering, grizzly eyes chased us all the way down Lexington Avenue. The street sweeping machine's beastly gyrating arms brushed us aside like a pile of trash.

(Sees treadmill and screams. To DIANA)

Hells bells, holy blazes, heaven help us, we care not a whit if you are the New Woman of 1912. Lady Birdwhistle wants this deathtrap out of this house!

(Kicks treadmill, hurting her foot.)

Out out damn spot! Out, tread machine, out, wash machine, out, wheat machine—euphemistakenly referred to as a 'toaster'. Burnt bread is not meant to fly across a room at breakfast! Lady Birdwhistle did not donate Father's specimens to the Museum of Natural History to have them replaced by the Museum of Manmade Horrors. Where will it end? Contraptions cooking supper, mechaniques performing medical exams, machines matchmaking the lovelorn? The last indignity we simply refuse to endure is that filthy, foul-smelling, frackish concoction recently poured inside our morning cup. The odor is reminiscent of a bodily function that shall remain unmentionable! The inventor of this Sanka decaffeinated devil's brew should be shamed, chastised, shot for his act of aggression against the civilized world!

THE BLAMELESS

Nick Gandiello

Seriocomic
Theresa, seventeen

Theresa is speaking to her mother, Diana. She and her Mom have just gotten into a nasty fight in which Theresa called their home "disgusting." The fight was fueled by Theresa having been caught in a compromising situation with her boyfriend, Howard. But the deeper problem of the night is that their family is preparing to meet the father of the young man who murdered Theresa's brother, Jesse.

THERESA

Mom I'm sorry, I'm really sorry. I said that before, it's just I get so exhausted, I get so exhausted trying to figure out if, if, if, if what I'm feeling, if what I'm feeling is, is, is because I'm grieving, if it's because like I'm bereaved, or if it's something I woulda felt anyway, if it's something I woulda felt if Jesse hadn't died, if Jesse hadn't died, ya know, like, like, like sometimes I get so angry at you, sometimes I get so angry at you, and would I have felt that, would I have felt that if Jesse was still here? Like would I love Howard so much, would I love him so much if Jesse had never died. So sometimes when you, when you, when you impose on me, when you impose on me that I have to be grieving, that what I'm doing must be because I'm grieving, it makes me, it makes me, it makes me feel resultant, it makes me feel resultant, and I don't want my life to be a result. I don't want forever, whenever I meet someone forever or do something forever to be the girl whose brother died in the school shooting!

(A pause, in which it seems she has gotten it all out. Then:)

And you know what Mom, you know what Mom, I did some stupid fucking shit today and it wasn't my like smartest move, it wasn't my like proudest moment, and ya know what, ya know what, maybe I did pick this day, like subconsciously, like unconsciously, like to, like to sabotage myself and get in trouble so I don't have to be here for this, so I don't have to be here while this guy is here because honestly what is this? Like this guy is gonna, gonna, what, sit here and, and, and no you know what, you know what, it wasn't subconscious, it wasn't unconscious, I didn't have rehearsal today and Howard didn't have jazz band and

(Whispering, but losing the intensity:)

sometimes I wanna give my boyfriend a blowjob and it's not because I'm a victim, it's not because I'm victimized, it's because I enjoy doing it, okay, I enjoy it. It isn't because I feel neglected. No one neglects me, no one ever neglects me, everyone is always staring at me waiting for me to have a breakdown or say something meaningful, I *wish* someone would neglect me, I *wish* someone would neglect me for five minutes. But, but, I dunno, maybe I did do it because today is today, I don›t know, maybe I did, maybe I did, because honestly, honestly, Mom, no one asked me if I was cool with Jacob Davis›s father being in our house, no one asked me if I was cool with that, it was just all of a sudden happening, and I don›t think I am, I don›t think I am cool with it!

BLUE LILA RISING

Sheila Callaghan

Dramatic
Dawn, forty

*Struggling novelist Dawn Powell is enduring a lavish cocktail party at
her agent's extravagant flat in Manhattan in 1936. There she meets the
hostess's clerk, Lilla (twenties). Lilla seems strikingly familiar to Dawn,
but she can't place how or from where she knows her. Lilla identifies herself
as a fan of Dawn's writing, especially her most recent manuscript, which
is different from the ones she's written before. A few moments later, Lilla
drops dead. No one seems to care about Lilla's death but Dawn. In this
monologue, Dawn eulogizes Lilla and takes responsibility for her demise.
Lilla represents Dawn's artistic struggle as she forces herself to move away
from 'rural middle class' stories she's passionate about to those of 'modern
urban living' in the hopes of finding success in her career. By forcing Lilla
to become someone she is not, she has essentially killed her muse.*

DAWN

Lila
you are a fog
you are everywhere I turn
you roll in from the sea
and lay a fine mist on my cheek
then you dissolve.

I dreamed of you before you were born.
You wore a tiara.
You floated.
You turned stars into laughter.

Your book, Lila
I fed it slowly
gave it milk ·
felt it full and glistening as it grew
with you its liquid center
brave and generous you
your toes ticking time to the

brilliant New York night
your heart drenched in longing
as the sky ripened around you

But the city feasted on my fascination
and gorged itself
the book was birthed
saturated with glamour and alacrity
and the vast and virile electric horizon
but you were lost.

My beautiful city devoured you.
I might have stayed its hand
I might have shaped your curves first
then allowed the flesh of New York to creep in
and settle against your outline

I might have
if the garden of lights hadn't
filled me first

The blood from your mouth
is on my hands, Lila

I want to undo this.
I want to take the book
press my hand through the pages
until my fingers feel the last moist morsel of you
drag you back through its spine
and tear you into the air
watch your blue dress fan out like fury around you
your long blue arms angled at the stars
your longing tangled around your tongue
your teeth bared your breath mint blue
and your body stretching until you are whole again
until your fingers burn
until the jewel in your tiara glows blue

BREATHING TIME

Beau Willimon

Dramatic
Julie, thirties

Julie's husband Mike died on 9-11. A co-worker's sister has tracked her down.

JULIE

I'm not even sure what Mike *did* at the office. Numbers I guess. Something to do with numbers and equations and—you know what? I hated the suit he was wearing in that picture. *Hated* it. It wasn't the right color on him at all. I said "Mike—take it back. Return it. I'll pick out something better for you, because you look *terrible* in navy blue, but he wouldn't listen to me. He *insisted* on wearing it. Just like his stupid car. He wouldn't listen to me about that either. "We can afford something better," I'd say—like a Lexus or an Audi, but he refused to give up his Volvo. Said it was a good sturdy car. "But it's rusting," I'd say, "it's falling apart. We don't want to be driving Todd around in something like that." "No no, it's fine. No sense spending all the money on a new car when we've got a perfectly good one." But it made me sick. To watch him drive away in that car every morning. It looked so *pathetic.* And then—then I got a call from the owners of the parking garage. "Can you please come pick up your car?" "I don't want it," I told them, "You can keep it, sell it for scrap, I don't care." "We don't want to pay for the tow truck," they say. So what I could I do? I came into the city and got the damn thing. Walked into the garage and there it was, completely covered in dust. All these cars covered with dust that no one had come to pick up. Couldn't they have washed them? Hosed them down? Done something? They expected *me* to wipe off all that dust? What in God's name were they thinking? This—you know - I really don't think this was a good idea.

For information on this author, click on the WRITERS tab at
www.smithandkraus.com.

BYHALIA, MISSISSIPPI

Evan Linder

Dramatic
Laurel, twenty-five - thirty-five

Laurel has recently given birth. Clearly, her husband Jim is not the father,
because the baby is black. The principal at the school where she teaches,
whose name is Paul, is the father. Here, she explains to Jim what happened.

LAUREL

I'm telling you my way Jim, so don't interrupt me. That's my rule.
Sit. *(Pause)* Last summer, when you told me about that girl in New Or-
leans, you'd already figured everything out. There was nothing for me
to do. You were gonna quit H&H so you wouldn't travel anymore,
you offered to set up meetings with Dr. Bannon at the church, you
were sincere when you apologized, you came clean about it to my
mother which wasn't even above and beyond, it was just dumb and I
bet you're still regretting that to this day. But I knew why you did all
that. You'd messed up and you knew it and you felt, not even bad, it
was like you were destroyed because of it. And I think what scared
me was how quickly I forgave you. And I did Jim, yes I remember
the crying and the screaming but I also remember telling you we'd
get through it. I remember us doing it on this couch that night. That
night Jim. Tears in our eyes and I let you inside me . . . I forgave you.
Fully and simply and pretty damn fast. And it wasn't even cause I
thought it was my duty to forgive you as your wife, because believe
me that is what I was taught. My momma taught me that. Except
she just taught me that you were supposed to ignore it, because that's
what she always did with my daddy. You just didn't give me a chance
to ignore it. And knowing that I loved you that much, that there was
no question in my mind that I was gonna forgive you . . . it was one
of the most precious moments of my life. It was as precious as the
first time I met you tailgating with Karl in the Grove and you made
fun of me for drinking Boone's Farm. It was as precious as the first
time you kissed me. It was precious. Because as mad as I was, I knew
I loved you enough that I would I'd never be able to imagine my life
without you. The kids we would have, the house we wanted to build,
everything. That was our plan. You were my plan. But I still had this

rage that would pop up when I'd least expect it, so during summer session last year, I finally let myself talk about it to someone. The rage. You're going to have to forgive me Jim. Because I made a mistake, and I did something wrong. Very wrong. Forget Paul, forget Ayesha, this ain't about them right now. It's me and you. It's us and that new baby, and I have to tell you Jim I already love him. I do, it was immediate, it was love at first sight. That ain't changing. So what is it going to take for you to forgive me?

For information on this author, click on the WRITERS tab at
www.smithandkraus.com.

BYHALIA, MISSISSIPPI

Evan Linder

Dramatic
Ayesha, twenty-five - thirty-five, African American

Ayesha's husband has fathered a child with Laurel, a teacher at his school. Here she confronts Laurel, whom she has known since they were kids.

AYESHA

I was always kind. Kinder than you. Even when we were little, I was kinder, I was smarter and I worked harder. Wasn't as pretty as you when we were growing up, but I knew there was nothing I could do about that. So I was kind. My mom taught me that was always the most important thing and I believed her too. Even when Sandy Fowler spent ten years calling me Puff. From third grade on, Puff the Magic Dragon. Wasn't my fault that's how my mom did my hair. Even after I got to have it straightened for my birthday in seventh grade, she never stopped calling me that. All the way until graduation. The point is I never did a goddamn thing to her and I didn't deserve it. So here's the truth Laurel. I don't deserve what you've done to me. I know I'm a sinner too, I'm not perfect. I hate admitting this, but when I moved up here to be with Paul, there was something in me that liked knowing that Jim couldn't really hold a job. I liked knowing y'all lived here when Paul and I were building our new house, knowing that working two times harder than you ever did had paid off. That being kind paid off. May not've been Christian, but it's the truth. I'm telling you the truth right now Laurel. Somebody needs to. You were a coward and I don't deserve this. Paul does. But I don't and my kids don't either.

For information on this author, click on the WRITERS tab at
www.smithandkraus.com.

CAUGHT

Christopher Chen

Dramatic
Wang Min, thirties

Wang Min, a conceptual artist, is talking about her theater/art hybrid piece to a journalist during an interview.

WANG MIN

America places a high premium on "truth." No persons of any other culture get more defensive when questioned over their "truth." This piece of journalism must be absolutely, empirically *true*. This piece of art must be emotionally *truthful*. So when a glitch in "truth" occurs, the impulse is to defend and argue your own "rules of truth" to the death. And in the meanwhile the real *content* of truth- workers' conditions in China- gets sidelined in the conversation. This is what captured my imagination- how arcane American truth battles reveal the hollowness of her global outreach. So Mike Daisey is a theater artist; and as per his perceived rules of his medium, he allows himself to stretch truth in order to craft a compelling narrative. But when placed in the context of NPR and This American Life, he runs into problems. Different medium, different rules. There has been a lot of this. Take James Frey for example, who is crucified by Oprah for his book *A Million Little Pieces. Again*, a confusion of category- if he had called it a *fictional* memoir, no problem. Non fiction? Big problem. What interests me is this rift that occurs when different sets of rules bump against each other. We open a great chasm of unknowing. We see we do not know anything other than the architecture of our own rules. So it is this rift I seek by mixing theater with visual art. The dislocation is set in motion from before the beginning, with publicity. The piece was advertised in both visual art and theater circles, so this current audience is from two worlds, each with distinct sets of expectations. Theater audiences may want things to move more quickly art patrons may want more private processing time. Both groups will be confounded by the blend that confronts them. The confusion begins when you enter the room. Are you supposed to sit or stand? When is the "show" going to start? Or has the "show" already begun"? We move forward to the "show's" beginning. Again, a confounding of mediums. A man speaks from a podium. It is a pre-emptive book tour, but with shades of a TED talk, and yet the whole thing is a "theatre monologue," delivered by an actor, *and* we are in an art gallery. We have four different mediums bouncing off each other. What do we hold on to? His story? And yet in the second temporal phase, his story is negated. More confusion. It is absolute chaos. Art patrons will cling to my visual art for dear life, theater patrons will hold desperately to familiar theater tropes. It helps to have recruited an extraordinary group to theater artists- a playwright, director, actors- to create material based on my prompts; this may give a fleeting sense of familiarity. Yet at our core we are working in tandem to undermine each other. And so we arrive now at the third temporal phase of the piece, where the artist is interviewed. Here, through our conversation, we hope to break any remaining authoritative bonds of appropriation, in order to move into a more foundational realm of truth.

CHARM
Philip Dawkins

Dramatic
Victoria, twenty-three, African American heterosexual, cis-gender
   female. Experiencing homelessness.

*Here, Victoria explains to her etiquette teacher and mentor why she and
her cis-gender husband, Donnie have been attending Mama's class which
was designated for the trans community.*

VICTORIA

I think Donnie tryin' to go back to prison. To be with his girlfriend. To be
with Nikki. That's her name. Or *his* name, I don't know the right word.

   [Beat.]

See, everybody just think Donnie and me come to Charms cuz a the
free food sometimes, but ... we go cuz Donnie—Cuz my husband
in love with—I mean she ain't like you, Mama, she ain't had all the
surgeries and everything, but I seen her picture. She real pretty, Mama.
She real pretty. It's okay, I mean, he didn't know. Before he went in,
he didn't—He really did love me for real—he *do* love me for real.
You can't *tell* nobody neither, you gotta swear you won't tell nobody.
Cuz like, in *our* hood, where we from, if anybody found out Donnie
in love with a—it just a lot safer if it look like he still love me. I can
protect him. He my best friend. Shit, he my only friend. I try to be
real nice to people, I think that's important. But I got my kids to take
care of, and Donnie to take care of, and we still tryna get us a place
to live. 'Sides. he say Nikki got at least three more years if she good,
five if she bad. And I think she pretty bad. At least he told me. Soon
as he got out. You know how many girls got HIV from they man on
the DL? Donnie ain't play me like that. He told me straight.

   (She giggles in spite of herself.)

Well, not *straight*. I thought comin' a Charms could help us with our
"situation," you know? Now, here you are bein' so nice to me, tryna
help me get a job and a place to stay and get my kids back. And Donnie just tryna—What if he do somethin' stupid just to go back? What
if he give up on me? Cuz why would he stay with—?

(She's gonna cry, but nope she pulls it together. A strong front.)

Not aw. It don't matter. I ain't givin' up on him. He *got* me, I am *with* him. That is for *real*.

I just wish there was somebody I was enough for.

CLOSED WINDOWS, OPEN DOORS

Glenn Alterman

Seriocomic
Jane, thirties - forties

Jane is seated next to Bob in his car. She has been madly in love with him for many years and this is their first date, finally. She is desperately trying to maintain her composure.

JANE

It's all like predetermined, preordained, whatever you want to call it, Bob. Everyone knows it; ya learn it in Life 101. There are no accidents, no, none! Not even here, in small town U.S.A. We bump, melt, merge, whatever you want to call it Bob, with people we are meant to meet, MEANT-TO-MEET! I believe that, I do. Really! I mean think about it, just think about it Bob! Fact that you're here, I'm here, and we're both sitting in your car, front of my house, ready to go, night on the town. No accident, no-no, none! No mistake. Preordained! And I want you to know, want you to know Bob, I was thrilled when you called last week. Surprised, thrilled, yeah! Thought, oh my God, Bob, BOB, imagine! After all these years! Not that I was sitting by the phone, no. I'm so busy at the library these days; non-stop, go-go-go. Books back and forth; library lunacy! Actually, you're lucky you got me in. Lucky I was even home. Luck, lucky, preordained! *(Pause)* But … but, it certainly was a surprise. 'Mean after all these years of seeing you at the supermarket, passing you on the street, seeing you drive by. Certainly was a surprise. And now, here, the two of us, sitting in your car, waiting … waiting *patiently*, may I add, for you put the key in the ignition so we can go somewhere and … So why don't you start the car, Bob? Y'know, the car can't start by itself. We can't go anywhere just sitting here.

CONFEDERATES

Suzanne Bradbeer

Seriocomic
Maddie, twenty-one, white.

Maddie and Will were at arts camp together when they were kids. Maddie had a crush on Will then, and she still has a crush on him now. In this monologue, Maddie is confiding in Will, heedless of the fact that he is now a reporter and she is the daughter of a candidate for president—because to her—Will remains the kid she had a crush on all those years ago. Maddie's tendency to speak before she thinks will get her in trouble. Also, Maddie is white and Will is black.

MADDIE

It's, like, the cult of identity, the idea that you have to have personal experience—direct personal experience—to have any authenticity in the subject of your art. See, originally, I wanted to do this art project on Harriet Tubman, but my advisor didn't think I should pursue it because it wasn't *authentic* coming from me. 'Cause I'm not, you know, black. And I just think that's crap. I mean, you shouldn't have to be African American to respond to Harriet Tubman! But Marion says—that's my advisor—and honest to God, I don't even know how she got the job. She's the chairman of the department and she's incompetent. Incompetent. Anyway, then idiot Marion throws Kara Walker at me, which, you know, I *love* Kara Walker, I *idolize* her—those silhouettes depicting slaves and slave life, the way they're all caricatured and mythic because she wants us to think about history and point of view, I mean, she's like my favorite artist! On the planet! But because Marion is black and, and okay, it's not that Marion's an idiot—in fact, she's definitely *not* an idiot—she's just incredibly politically correct and boring. And her point is that Kara Walker can create art about slavery because Kara Walker is black. But what does Kara Walker know about being a slave? She doesn't know any more about it than I do—I have an imagination too, I've completely studied the subject too—we're both just nice middle class girls who grew up in the South. And yeah, one of us happens to be—a *genius*. But I can aspire to that, right? If no one aspired to great things because 'oh, so and so did it better'—where would we be? In the caves! We'd still be in the caves! So then I'm like, okay *Marion,* you don't want me to do a project on Harriet Tubman? Fine, I'll do a project on *you* not wanting *me* to do Harriet Tubman!

LAWRENCE HARBISON

THE COWARD

Kati Schwartz

Comic
Amelia, eighteen

Just out of high school, Amelia is an over-eager, excitable musical theater fanatic. Here, she has just been introduced to her fellow summer theater actors, and speaks to them about her favorite musical, Legally Blonde.

AMELIA

Legally Blonde!! *(Pause for dramatic effect).* Let me start with this: there has never been so much drama onstage or off! *(With exuberant gestures)* It was like a nuclear explosion of crazy!! I saw that show on Broadway like every day. There was so much *drama,* stupid drama. I love drama, and it was even stupid for me. It's like one of those things I look back on and it's like, that wasn't real. It was weird shit. And like this is on *Broadway.* I'm *such* a musical theater person!! During *Legally Blonde*, my friend Eva was in it, she understudied Elle, and she only went on *tuuu-wice.* Ever. Which is bad because she was the best ever. She is amazing, and I'm not just saying that because I know her. She was incredible. She kicked *butt.* She's one of the people that inspired me to start working out. Um, so we found out that she was going on for Elle, and me and some of my friends and other people who were just fans of the show or whatever camped out over night to get tickets. We slept in front of the Palace Theater, which is right in Times Square. For twelve hours we were there. And it was absolutely freezing, but so much fun. And at like three A.M. we decided that we wanted to perform *Legally Blonde* on the street, at a full belt, in Times Square! *(Dramatic pause)* So we did! We performed all of *Legally Blonde*! It was so fierce! Also a very drunk lady dropped her pizza on us and she was like *(slurred)* "shiiiiiit." She was smashed. It was awesome.

For information on this author, click on the WRITERS tab at
www.smithandkraus.com.

THE COWARD

Kati Schwartz

Seriocomic
Jill, twenty-three

Jill is a bright and naïve young woman with a vivid imagination and a strong connection to all things fantastical. Here, she speaks to the director of the summer theater she's working for. She has endured bullying from her close-minded roommate, and is hoping to be moved to a new room for the remainder of the summer.

JILL

This story is actually hilarious. I was at theater school in New York City. I was twenty-one and had never been kissed. There was this girl, Fiona, who was tall, blonde, Australian, and, it turns out, completely evil. And I was in love with her. Which was, like, weird for me. The winter of that year, we had a Christmas party. Leading up to this, Fiona had started spending more and more time with me. We met for coffee, got drinks, held hands when we walked. She asked me if I was a lesbian. Which, like, I said no. One day, we were out on a coffee date, and she leaned in and said . . . I want to kiss you. Is that weird? *(Pause)* I think I mumbled something awkward about how sexuality is fluid. It was pathetic how ecstatic I was. I was SO excited for my first kiss. I spent the entire week thinking and writing in my journal about it. I got a new dress at H&M . . . I even bought breath mints and put them in my purse. The night of the party came. After a few drinks and some dancing, I asked when the kiss was going to be. It was a set up. They just wanted to know if I was gay. Not only did I never get the kiss, but for the rest of the year, all nineteen of my class members, plus one of my teachers perpetuated the rumor that I was a sex predator against other women, until I had to drop out of school. *(Pause.)* But it's kind of funny right? I'm not telling you this story to make you feel bad for me, or anything. It's hilarious if you think about me being a sex predator, right? *(Silence)* I feel awkward because I can see you're taking this really seriously but like . . . I used to think it was a tragedy but its not. When this first happened, I would throw myself on the ground and sob for hours and feel like I wanted to die, and then I had this weird ethereal moment where I saw a birds eye view of myself thrashing around on the ground and it was hilarious. And then I realized it was a comedy, not a tragedy. It was funny! I promise you, it's . . . it's a comedy. It's not sad. Anyway, I don't know why I told you all of that . . . all I'm wondering is, can I move to a new room?

For information on this author, click on the WRITERS tab at www.smithandkraus.com.

DARN IT! DARLA!
Lavinia Roberts

Comic
Portia. Mid-thirties.

A now grown up childhood sitcom star, Naveen, (known for her charac-
ter, Darla Darling) is struggling to find meaningful work for women in
Hollywood. Portia, her manager, has some advice about how to revamp
her image.

PORTIA

Well, I think there might be a way to get you past bit parts in Lifetime original made-for-TV movies, guest appearances on daytime soaps, and late night infomercials. We need to give you a new image, bring you back into the public's view. How do you feel about drunk driving? Embezzling money. A new nose, maybe bigger breasts? Have you ever thought about developing an eating disorder? Maybe being found with a couple grams of cocaine? You would only have to be in jail for a few months. Just long enough for all the paper headlines to read, "Darn it Darla; not so Darling anymore!" Start a charity or something? Human beings are only salacious morsels and fallible weakness. We don't want our leaders to talk about our troubles. We want them to be HD ready. We don't want to know about the state of the ozone or economy. But who looks best in a bikini after having a baby, and who has cellulite and where. Do a public service. Give them someone to hate for a while. They'll never know you or be you, but it makes them feel big for a moment to feel better then you. They'll love to hate you. And they'll cough up the change the next time your on the big screen, just so they can complain about you afterwards to their companions. All I'm asking for is some much needed plastic surgery, a little jail time, to become bulimic, maybe to spend a little time addicted to cocaine, so you can go to rehab? That's all. What manager could be more concerned for your well-being?

For information on this author, click on the WRITERS tab at
www.smithandkraus.com.

DAUGHTERS OF THE SEXUAL REVOLUTION

Dana Leslie Goldstein

Dramatic
Judy, thirty

Judy is trying to convince her therapist that she no longer needs to be taking valium. The year is 1976.

JUDY

I wasn't always like this. I was a calm child. That's what my mother says. But then I started to worry about the world. That's not crazy. It's a worrisome place, the world. They're still shooting at each other in Cambodia. And we're commemorating a battle right here. I know it isn't patriotic to say it, but this bicentennial business is making me—edgy. Ricky came home last week with an assignment to dress as a colonial … something. A founding father, that kind of thing. Liam made him a musket out of plywood, not one that really shoots of course, but it was a weapon, it was a commemoration of killing, and I didn't say anything. I should have. But I didn't. Ricky brought it to school, and an older kid took it away from him. And he hit another kid with it. Not Ricky. The older kid—maybe ten or eleven years old - hit some other kid he'd had a fight with the day before. Nothing to do with the bicentennial, it was just the best weapon at hand. And this other kid needed stitches. And the musket was taken away. And this is—this is in what was supposed to be the safest town in the safest suburb of yes, an unsafe city, but still - most people in this country don't live anywhere this safe. And most people in this world—well —forget about them, it's no contest - But I can't forget about them. I can't—get them or Ricky or any of this out of my head. And I know it's not the bicentennial's fault, I'm not crazy. But it feels like it is. Why do we need countries anyway? They just lead to more - Maybe if I went back to work, I'd stop worrying so much. I could teach or - Liam wants to have another baby. I can't do that. I can't! I'm all wound up again. I didn't mean to get like this. I don't get like this, usually. At least, I didn't used to. I told Liam it's the valium. He says that's ridiculous. I don't want to take it any more. So I—I don't. Every so often, I just don't take it. And then I can't sleep. Or I get like this. I don't want to get like this. It's worse than when I started on it. I never should've started on it. *(pause)* How do I get back there? To before? That's what I want out of this. Out of these sessions. I want to go back in time. You can't help with that, can you? It's too late for me. But Ricky - He was innocent before Liam put that gun in his hand. He's losing that—he's eight years old, and he's losing his innocence. I have to make that stop.

For information on this author, click on the WRITERS tab at www.smithandkraus.com.

DINNER AT HOME BETWEEN DEATHS

Andrea Lepcio

Dramatic
Lily, twenties

Lily is speaking to Sean. She has reluctantly shown up for a quasi-inter-view. She has been sent by her former step-mother, long divorced from her adoptive father. She let Kat send her because she has just gotten out of rehab and is hungry for something else in a life that has so far only been wealthy, empty and boring. She knows that Sean is famous for his stock prediction model. She thinks maybe she wants in. She is trying to impress him, something she's never tried in life.

LILY

I like math. I'm good at it. I was good at it. I haven't done anything harder than addition, subtraction, not even long division, since Dalton. But, I was good at math. Like differential calculus. Algebra's deadly dull. As if x were a finite thing. I mean. *She checks if he is listening. He is.* I liked finding the equation, like an arrow, aimed at the answer. Solving for how one thing changes the thing changing it. And then using that equation to draw the curve of the change, The damage, The inevitable. All my life I was like what the fuck? It felt like there were no answers anywhere, no explanation for anything. The catastrophe that was my parentals. Suddenly these equations making curves with the whole of life riding under them. So like even if today sucks there is this infinite place where answers are possible. Even if it's never here Never where I am. It's there at the end the place the arrow will stab infinitely.

DINNER AT HOME BETWEEN DEATHS

Andrea Lepcio

Dramatic
Lily, twenties

Lily is speaking to Sean. This monologue appears in the play after Sean has killed her. The audience knows she is dead and that Sean is guilty. It appears around when the other two characters are finding out. The timing of the monologue is a few months into Lily working for and sleeping with Sean. She is liking the work very much and the sex well enough. This is as content as she has ever been in life.

LILY

I hate people. Not you. I kind of do love some people. Not you. But I hate, people. Don't trust the way they intrude. When you're a child, you have no control over the intrusion. Or the neglect. The places people press into you, the places they fall away. I was like 13. 8th grade. New school. What parent changes your school in the middle of middle school? Example. So, like, I'm 13 going on nine. And all these kids at this new school are like 14 going on 36. They're like drinking and fucking. Fucking, not groping. And raiding their parents medicine cabinets. And I'm the new kid. And I don't have a frame of reference. But I'm like exotic. They're white except one scholarship student. And they make me their friend. Like all of the popular kids decide on mass they want me. So I'm like in. And pretty quickly I decide I hate beer and vodka, and pretty quickly I decide fucking 14 year old boys is lame, and pretty quickly I decide Valium is my homeroom. The first thing, the only thing that made the places where people press in calm, made the places where they fall away not ache. Thanks a lot, rehab—one day at a time, realigned expectations, people still suck, live and let live rehab We have endless expressions Take what you like and leave the rest. I leave a lot But I take this. I like this.

DRAW THE CIRCLE

Mashuq Mushtaq Deen

Dramatic
Lucia, forties, Latina

Lucia is talking to her friends. She was the first person to talk to Shireen, a transgender friend, after Shireen's suicide attempt. Lucia has never seen Shireen before, and never will again.

LUCIA

This one day I'm changing a room like I always do, I've got my vacuum cleaner, I've got my Lysol, I'm listening to my *boleros* on my headphones, when what do I see on the TV but an envelope! An envelope, like the kind of envelopes that people leave tips in!— I know, right? Nobody tips in this shithole!—So my heart stops and I think—*Dios Mio, Muchas Gracias!*—because we need the money. But, there is no money. It's a letter and you can't believe what it said: "DEAR FAMILY & FRIENDS, THIS IS MORE THAN I CAN BEAR AND I CAN'T MAKE IT GO AWAY. I'M STAYING ALIVE FOR OTHER PEOPLE AND IT'S NOT ENOUGH ANYMORE. I JUST WANT TO GO HOME. I'M SORRY—I WISH YOU ALL THE STRENGTH I NEVER HAD. GOODBYE. SHIREEN DEEN" Then, this young Indian-looking girl appears in the doorway, and she's like, oh shit, because she knows that I know, and how can I not know, she has a bandage on her wrist, and I'm not stupid. So I say her name, like it's signed at the bottom of the letter—SHIREEN DEEN? It's her. In my head I heard *mi Mama* carrying on about sinners and hell, but curiosity got the best of me, and you wouldn't believe it, but I asked her, What did you do? And she says to me, she came to Deerfield to do her laundry. When her laundry was done she had a meal. When the meal was done, she wrote a letter. When the letter was done, she broke an ashtray and tried to go Home." So I said, Home? Where do YOU live? And she says, "With God." And then she says, she let everyone go, everyone she loves—Dr. Erikson, Dr. Masters, her parents, everyone. And she cut vertically, like you're supposed to, and she tried to keep it in the sink so I wouldn't have too much to clean up. She squeezes the bandage on her wrist. Then she says, But she couldn't cut deep enough, and it was because there was this little voice inside her soul and it was God, and, and not for anyone else, but for God, she'll try this life thing one more time. Because God will punish you? I asked. And she shook her head and said, To know that someone loves her that much, that unconditionally, she feel like maybe she can do the impossible. Live.

ELLERY

Jennifer O'Grady

Seriocomic
Liesel, twenty-four

Liesel is a psychic who has secretly harmed her best friend in order to advance her own career. She is speaking to the audience.

LIESEL *(to Audience)*

Okay. So sue me. Do you have any idea what it's like being me?

(to an Audience member)

Well, maybe *you* do. But the rest of you don't. *(Beat)* People are always thinking you're fucked up, or off your meds. Even when you try to hide it. But we can't hide anything from *them*. They *know*. Every try to ignore someone who's yakking at you ceaselessly? And believe me, the dead can talk. They don't have anything else to do. *(Pause)* And holding down a job? Forget it. If you work in some old building, chances are someone had a heart attack there, or fell down a flight of stairs. Even in a brand-new building, because who knows what was there first? Might have been some orphanage, or a cemetery. *(Pause)* I don't know why I was born like this. I would have been happy being an archaeologist. But an archaeological dig isn't the best place for a sensitive. Ever try listening to more than ten people at a time? And the dead always want something. *(Beat)* I have to pay my rent somehow. I live in a capitalistic, entrepreneurial society. If I don't take care of *me,* then nobody will. And right now, I'm alive.

For information on this author, click on the WRITERS tab at
www.smithandkraus.com.

THE ETRUSCAN LOVERS

C.S. Hanson

Seriocomic
Mimi, mid- to late-thirties, curator of Etruscan art.

The setting is a gallery in a metropolitan art museum. It's the night of the Annual Patron's Gala. Mimi wants to lure patrons to her the gallery in hopes of saving the statue of the Etruscan Lovers from being returned to Italy (from where it was stolen years ago). She tries to seduce a wealthy patron, Lance Worth, into falling in love with the sculpture. Little does she know that he's a former art thief.

MIMI

I fell in love with the Etruscans when I was in college. But I have to blame D.H. Lawrence for that. I read everything I could find by him, including a curious book called "Etruscan Places." It's considered light reading among scholars. But it's beautiful and it captures their essence. They were creative and inventive, but most of all, life was to be enjoyed. There I was, reading about men and women in 600 B.C., and I wanted what they had. I went to Italy, saw the tombs—wonderful sunken places cut out of rock, underground. Filled with fading scenes of how they lived day to day. I discovered, in the tombs, a sense of who I really was—or wanted to be. I embraced the creed of the Etruscans, that death was a grand continuation of life, to be viewed as a celebration. Their underworld is a very lively place. Full of music and dancing and all the things they enjoyed in this world. I'll let you touch them if you want. To connect with another time and culture, I believe you must immerse yourself in it. Sometimes that means touching, or at least getting close. I'm an Etruscan, after all! And you are too. Yes. You are. Dance with me.

FABULOUS MONSTERS

Diana Burbano

Dramatic
Slade, sixties

Slade (aka Sally Rodriguez) is a hard living, seen it all punk rocker from the 70's, alive, sober and cynical as hell.

SLADE

I've read a ton of books describing the whole Punk scene, ya know? But, the ones writing the history are the poser assholes who made it out alive. And it's like, a mandate, to slag people off. 'specially women like Patti and Debbie. Jesus, when don't you read that Debbie «got fat?» Everyone «got fat,» man. We had no money to buy food, what money we had we spent on drugs, and one show burnt about a million calories. Start acting like a norm, and the weight piles on pretty fast. I recently saw a guy I knew walking outside what used to be Ed's in DTLA. He lived in a loft, but not one of those yuppified Toy District lofts, he lived in a flophouse on the edge of Chinatown. The place was CRAMMED with junk. Clothes in piles to the ceiling. Cat shit everywhere. He had 3 gold records covered in dust and God knows what. He spends most of his time in bed playing Call of Duty. Fat. We're all fat and poor now, man. We signed away every right we had. This shit just fizzles out. You're young, you play your guts out. You spark, someone wants to record you! You tour, you cut an album. Path diverges: You burn out and go back to school. Or you die of an overdose. Or you tour some more. Path diverges. Touring sucks so you quit. You kill yourself. Or you cut another album. No one buys it. You quit and go do something else. Or you kill yourself. Ad infinitum. It›s either death or normality. If you are the one half of the one percent who keeps going it›s 'cause you're fucking crazy.

FABULOUS MONSTERS

Diana Burbano

Dramatic
Slade, sixties

Slade (aka Sally Rodriguez) *is a hard living, seen it all punk rocker from the 70's, alive, sober and cynical as hell.*

SLADE

So many of us are dead. Yeah, lots of OD's but you don't necessarily die 'cause of the drugs themselves. You choke on a sandwich. Or your puke. You drown in your bathtub. You slice your arm open on the glass you threw and bleed out 'cause you're too high to notice. OR you top yourself. Hanging is popular. It's fairly simple and self explanatory, and if you are high while doing it it doesn't feel so bad. Cutting is harder, but only because human flesh is surprisingly tough. Shooting yourself, or your girlfriend. Stabbing your girlfriend. That was like a theme. I knew someone who ate glass. That didn't work so much. Drinking weed killer works but rots your insides slowly, so the death is agony. Disease killed a lot of us. AIDS mostly. No surprise how many people we lost, but MAN some people must've had immune systems of iron to get out alive. Bowie and Iggy. How the FUCK did they survive intact? Lessee . . . I knew a girl who was eaten by her cats, but we think she died from an OD first. Sometimes I get together with friends from the early days and we try to figure out how many of our friends are dead. Last time we stopped counting at 57. It was too fucking depressing. Now that we're old, cancer is eating up a lot of us. The chicks seem to get a lot of breast cancer. But that's possibly just the population at large and rock chicks aren't special. Or maybe our guitars are fucking us up.

A FUNNY THING HAPPENED ON THE WAY TO THE GYNECOLOGIC ONCOLOGY UNIT AT MEMORIAL SLOAN-KETTERING CANCER CENTER OF NEW YORK CITY

Halley Feiffer

Seriocomic
Karla, twenty-something

In a shared hospital room where both of their mothers are being treated for cancer, Karla develops a peculiar connection with Don, a middle-aged divorced man. Karla has just learned that Don is wealthy, despite his ill-fitting, destitute attire. The two of them talk while their mothers sleep.

KARLA

Oh, her insurance is _terrible_. Which is hilarious, 'cause she's a social worker. It's like, "Thanks for the help, U.S. Government!" _(Chuckles.)_ We're totally fucked. _(Laughs.)_ I should probably just kill myself. _(She laughs. A beat.)_ That was a joke. I'm not going to kill myself. _(Beat.)_ Today. _(Beat.)_ That was a _joke!_ God. You do not understand my charming and irreverent dark sense of humor at _all. (Beat.)_ I mean, we're not _fucked_, I was being dramatic. We're just—it's just ... . _(Beat.)_ I mean, her insurance is great in a lot of ways—they paid for her surgery and her week of recovery here which is awesome, but then when it comes to, like, the chemo and the radiation and the medications, it's just .... It's gonna be tougher. _(Beat.)_ But don't worry, Don. You looked so _worried_ right now. It's _fine_. This is how the world _works_. Shit happens, and you just—you figure it out. Or ... you don't. You just accept that life is ... kind of shitty. And that's okay. And maybe it'll change. Or maybe it won't. And that's okay too! Or maybe it's not. And maybe it's okay that it's not okay. You know? _(Beat.)_ No, of course you don't. You have like seven gajillion _dollars_, so if your mom dies, you can just, like ... buy a new one. _(Beat.)_ Sorry. That was another attempt at a dark joke and it ... yeah it wasn't the time. I acknowledge that. Timing is everything. _(In an old time-y vaudevillian voice.)_ "What is the secret to great comedy?" TIMING!

For information on this author, click on the WRITERS tab at
www.smithandkraus.com.

A FUNNY THING HAPPENED ON THE WAY TO THE GY-NECOLOGIC ONCOLOGY UNIT AT MEMORIAL SLOAN-KETTERING CANCER CENTER OF NEW YORK CITY

Halley Feiffer

Comic
Karla, twenty-something

Short summary of dramatic context: Karla, a stand-up comedian, visits her cancer-ridden mother in the hospital. While her mom sleeps, Karla practices her jokes out loud, imagining that her mother—with whom she has a contentious relationship—is listening to and supporting her.

KARLA

(reading from a notepad)

"I've been single for so long? I've started having sexual fantasies about my vibrator." *(Beat.)* Now what do you think works better, "sexual fantasies" or "sex dreams"? Or *"wet dreams"?* I actually think "wet dreams" is the funniest option, but I'm worried it might not get a laugh because girls don't have wet dreams. *(Considers this.)* Per se … . *(Beat.)* Yeah, fuck it. Wet dreams? You're in. *(Scribbles in notepad.)* And I have more stuff I could add on to it, too—like I could elaborate even more? Like I could—oh Idunno this is all just *improv,* but like I could be like: "Instead of a strong, chiseled, oiled-up man throwing open my bedroom door and raping me? I just have visions of like, my vibrator standing in the archway, backlit by silvery moonlight, sometimes wearing a fedora *(sometimes not),* and lovingly fucking me 'til sunrise." *(Beat.)* What do you think of that? That was just improv. *(Beat.)* Maybe the rape part was a bit much. *(Scribbles in notepad.)* I don't know, I kinda don't think there's anything funnier than rape. *(Thinks.)* Okay, well what if I just said something like … "I'm in bed, dripping wet, waiting for my vibrator to come fuck me"? Maybe that's like—does that kinda take the teeth out of it, though? Am I being a pussy? Arghhh, I can never tell if I'm just resorting to being a big, gaping wide pussy. *(Beat.)* Or I could even work the rape element *into* it, but in like a different *way*—like I could say something like: "I love getting fucked by my vibrator 'cause I know it'll never rape me." *(Thinks.)* Or something like that. *(Scribbles in notepad.)* How about—ha ha—how about: "I only rape myself with my vibrator when I'm *really angry* at myself"? Too much? *(Scribbles in notepad.)* Okay here's a compromise: "I only play out my rape fantasies with my *vibrator*, 'cause I know it will always respect my safe word." *(Thinks.)* It's still maybe too vague . . . .

For information on this author, click on the WRITERS tab at
www.smithandkraus.com.

A FUNNY THING HAPPENED ON THE WAY TO THE GYNECOLOGIC ONCOLOGY UNIT AT MEMORIAL SLOAN-KETTERING CANCER CENTER OF NEW YORK CITY

Halley Feiffer

Seriocomic
Karla, twenty-something

A few days after Marcie's hospital roommate has died, Karla witnesses her mother in a moment of utter vulnerability —perhaps for the first time in her life. Unsure of what to do, Karla tries to tell her mother a story that she hopes will offer some comfort.

KARLA

Um so on my way over here? It was so funny because there was um this. Um. So I was on the 6 train? And it was really crowded and I was just like holding onto a pole and listening to music and just kinda zoned out because I was really tired? And um, then this, um—I had the music on *shuffle?* And then this, um, this . . . song came on? This song that, um. That Erika used to—do you remember? She used to play this song all the time? Really loud? Like on a loop? In her room? And my initial reaction was to be, like, oh *god*—let me switch the song, you know? 'Cause . . . Idunno, 'cause I guess when you hear a song that many times, you kind of . . . never need to hear it again? *(Laughs.)* And also 'cause . . . I don't know. 'Cause I guess it reminds me of . . . Erika? So. *(Beat.)* But then I just . . . keep listening. And then I just. Um. For some reason, I just. Like. Start crying? I mean I was standing on the subway holding onto a pole, sandwiched in between a gajillion strangers, like, *weeping. (Laughs.)* And then . . . someone taps me on the arm. And it's this total stranger—he's this short Latino dude with like these really thick glasses? And he has earbuds in, too. And he goes: *(She does a gesture with her hands to indicate swapping something.)*
And I'm like, "Uhhh . . . what?" And he does it again—*(Does the "swapping" gesture again.)* And then he starts to take out his earbuds. And so I take out mine. And then we just . . . swap. Earbuds. And I start listening to his music and he starts listening to mine. And his music is like . . . . it's like *the* worst Top 40 teeny-bopper power ballad? That I have legitimately ever heard. And I'm about to take his earbuds

out and be like: "Sorry dude, I can't." But then . . . I look up at him and he has my earbuds in and he goes: *(She imitates him—big grin, bopping to the music, giving a thumbs up sign.)* And I go: *(She does the same thing—smiles big, bops to the music and gives a thumbs up sign.)* And Mom? We rode the train like that? For *half an hour.*

(Beat; remembers.)

And then the train stops at 59th Street, and I realize that I have to get off at the next stop. So I start taking out his earbuds and he takes out mine—and we have said literally not one word to each other this entire time—and I give him back his earbuds and he gives me back mine. And the train slows down, and I'm about to get off, and I look at the guy, to be like, "Bye?" And he just . . . puts his hand on my shoulder. *(Beat.)* And he says . . . nothing. He just . . . looks at me. With his hand on my shoulder. And I look at him. And then . . . *(Beat.)* I get off the train.

For information on this author, click on the WRITERS tab at
www.smithandkraus.com.

GABRIEL (A Polemic)

C. Denby Swanson

Seriocomic
Susan, thirties

Susan, the bitter, prickly host of tonight's Sabbath evening potluck for her sisterhood of faith, has an agenda: Do we have free will?

SUSAN

The Sabbath happens once a week, like clock-work. Like Mah Jongg. Or Poker. Will you win the game this time? Will you be saved from your terrible debts? The Sabbath happens at sunset and, as you can see, the sun is going down. The holy moment has begun, the transition between light and dark has arrived. So this in fact is a perfect example of the issue of the evening, which is, of course, free will. Jennifer, you can stay remote and easily offended and even a little judge-y of the rest of the world; Brenda, you can continue your effort at the jigsaw puzzle of sisterhood and reconciliation using us as edge pieces even though we do not easily fit with each other. Or, together, we can serve the meal. And as you both know, the Sabbath meal must be served at dusk, in other words, it has to be served right now, and if we don't eat it we disobey God. If we don't eat it we violate our faith in him. The provider. The most high. The maker of heaven and earth. He giveth and he taketh away. Will you serve your leeks, Jennifer, and Brenda will you serve that potato thing that you bring every single time and which I'm sure you also learned to make from your grandmother, or, as a sign of your own willfulness, your own innate ability to decide for yourself, will you refuse to bring your dishes to the table and miss the blessed moment? Do you, in fact, have free will, meaning can you, will you, defy what God wants you to do? Or are you going to follow his will and cooperate so that we can have dinner, truly embodying his invective to serve your fellow man?

GABRIEL (A Polemic)

C. Denby Swanson

Dramatic
Brenda, thirties

Brenda is usually the meek one of her sisterhood of faith, but at tonight's Sabbath evening potluck she has something to say about free will and motherhood.

BRENDA

I need to say, I have something to say to Louise. God has put it on my heart. I think, what if, maybe the baby is a reward. I know. I know. It's awful. I know. But listen: A terrible thing and God loves us. A good thing and God loves us. There are a lot of, of issues I'm not certain about, I'm not as certain as you are, Susan, there are a lot of things I don't know, and don't know how to answer, and get wrong, and when I get them wrong I stumble more. And I find forgiveness in my faith. Sometimes. Mostly. I can see that Louise was violated and wounded and Susan was wounded also and I think, Praise God that one among us gets to have a baby. I'm sorry but that's what I think. And I do think that Mary chose, but like you said, Susan, if she could choose yes, then she could choose no. She just didn't. Which is hard to juggle in my head. Because I think about that, I think about it, and there are lots of ways, I just, I think about it, because the thing I am not sure about, the thing that causes me the most, I think if I knew I could be a mother I would be so much more certain about other things. I think I would just know. I would know my place, I guess. Maybe you don't. Maybe you know now, maybe you're more certain now, I just don't know my place right now and a baby, a child would—so I look at you, Louise, and I think, She has a place in the world, a firm and lasting and secure place in the world, with this new relationship. Everything happens for a reason.

GORGONS

Don Nigro

Seriocomic
Mildred, fifties

Mildred, an actress in her fifties, shows up at her rival Ruth's door very late at night after she's just been forced to hand over to her the Best Actress Oscar at the Academy Awards and then listen to a long self-promoting and falsely humble acceptance speech in which Ruth thanks half the people on the planet but neglects to mention Mildred. They made a horror movie together as a last attempt to keep their careers alive, and Ruth has somehow managed to fight her way to the award. Mildred, who considers herself a much more serious actress, is furious, and a bit drunk.

MILDRED

Congratulate you? You think I've come here to congratulate you? What kind of bizarre, sick fantasy world are you living in, anyway? I don't want to sit on the sofa. I want to sit on your face. You thank half the population of the civilized world, including a one-eyed Bulgarian grip who smells like a fart factory, your cat, Mr Poopy, and your stupid fucking cockatoos, and you don't even bother to mention my name? I want to thank Dopey and Sneezy and Bashful and Grumpy, and that left-handed soda jerk in Fresno, the hobo who shits on my lawn, Spike Jones, the Bobbsey Twins, Herbert Hoover—You mentioned every other person on the planet but me. You somehow screw me out of getting a nomination—all right, I can deal with that, you campaigned for it, I didn't—you put ads in the paper, I didn't, you've slept with the nominating committee, I didn't—I can understand that. Then you win—that I don't understand, but after all, these people are not mental giants, these are movie people, they have the brains of a kumquat and the morals of hyenas, but I can deal with that too, just barely, but I can deal with it. It's an occupational hazard to be periodically shat upon by cretins. But then, to have to go out there with a straight face and actually hand you the damned thing, and then stand there behind you smiling like an idiot and listen to you thank Coo Coo the cross-eyed makeup girl, your three-legged dog Tootsie and half the population of Madagascar—and then you don't even have the common decency to mention my name? You knew exactly what you were doing. You memorized that speech like it was the Gettsyburg Address. You choreographed every move like Nijinsky, down to the little tear that rolled down your cheek at the end. You practiced it in front of the mirror for weeks. And you did it all on purpose just to humiliate me. You rope me into doing this cockamamie piece of crap, nearly kill me in the process, win the fucking statue, presented to you by four or five hundred people you've fornicated with over the last century and a half, and then you don't even have the decency to mention my name along with Mr Poopy? I don't think you even have a cat. And do you know what the worst part is? The worst part is that I had finally allowed myself to believe that you were—that we had somehow, after all the shrieking and the backbiting, managed to connect, somehow, to understand one another, to actually, God help me, establish a sort of friendship. I've never had a friend. Isn't that pathetic? In my whole wretched life, I've never really had a friend to call my own. And yet, by the end there, I actually felt like you and I had bonded in some significant way, that perhaps only two old battle-axes like us could ever really understand what it took to become us, what we gave up to get to this place, the loneliness and the stored up resentment and jealousy and terror over all the years. I thought we actually, on some level, understood each other, communicated to one another in a relatively honest way. But it was all bullshit, wasn't it? It was all acting. It was acting. Ruth, you were acting. How COULD you?

GREEN-WOOD
Adam Kraar

Dramatic
Gretchen, thirty-three

Gretchen is in a cemetery in front of a wall of niches where ashes are stored. She has come to speak with her long-departed brother.

GRETCHEN

Hello, Robbie.

(She takes a can of Red Bull from her purse.)

I brought you this. Started to get you flowers, but then I could hear you—rolling your eyes.

(She puts the can on the ground in front of the niche, then looks again at her brother's niche.)

. . . .You were always like this. An edifice! Pretending I wasn't there? What was the deal with that? Afraid I'd somehow contaminate you with my nerdishness? Or somehow dismantle your Star Wars defenses against Mom and Dad? Didn't you know?? All I ever, ever wanted was to, like, be your friend . . . Sorry. I know you hate this. It's just: I always thought . . . you would be—my anchor. Well, maybe not my anchor but … I mean: You built rockets, you built a computer, you built a castle—to protect you from the mishegoss of our family. I looked up to you. You put training wheels on my bike—which nobody else would do. And then, when I tried to thank you, you just walked away. Well, now you can't walk away. You're stuck in that niche—or wherever you are.

(She turns away from the niche. Then, after a moment, turns back.)

You wouldn't recognize me. I'm not remotely a nerd. In college, I was considered hot. And you know what? I'm an archeologist. A professor at Cornell, specializing in Indonesia. I discovered a whole new layer of an ancient city in Java. I was on the cover of *Archeology News.* Yeah. *(pause)* Eleven years ago, I got married, but it only lasted a few months. Problem is, archeologists get too distracted by the past . . . I can tell you why an ancient Buddhist temple was abandoned in the

14th century. I can reconstruct everything that happened in the final years of a civilization, down to the season. But I can't—begin—to understand what ... What happened to you??

HOORAY FOR HOLLYWOOD!
Lisa Soland

Seriocomic
Peg Entwhistle, twenty-four

It is 1932, and Peg's hopes of becoming a Hollywood starlet have been dashed. She sits atop the "Hollywoodland" sign in the hills above Hollywood, trying to decide whether or not to jump.

PEG

Who in their right mind would name their daughter "Millicent?" What were you thinking, Robert and Emily? You, with such normal names. I'll use Peg. Peg Entwhistle will do just fine in this wonderful world of entertainment. And what a movie debut I had! "David O. Selznick's *Thirteen Women* starring Irene Dunne, Myrna Loy and Peg Entwhistle." A disaster, like everything I touch. Tell me now Swami, what swift doom do you see happening here this evening? Maybe I should write to you instead. You are real, aren't you? If you exist in a movie, you must be real. Was it you who planted this unthinkable thought into my mind? Jump. Jump. Stop talking yourself to death and jump. *(Beat.)* Movies may make you famous but it's the theatre that makes you good. The only acting that challenges—my one remaining hope—shattered. If they'd only responded in some way positive to my audition at the Beverly Hills Playhouse. Hell, I'm a shoe-in for the role of a woman who commits suicide, don't you think?

(Looks up to God.)

You who created me like this—tainted! Don't you think?! That part was mine and they did nothing but sit there with those two-faced-looks on their Beverly Hills faces, saying how much they loved me, but did I receive a notice? Any form of communication whatsoever? No. This town isn't meant for soft souls. How does Will Rogers do it? "I never met a man I didn't like." Liar! Just like everyone else in this town, says one thing but means something else entirely. *(Beat.)* This city—all glitz and glamour, but when you take away the lights, all you have is the cold, hard metallic letters that do nothing to sooth the dark and lonely emptiness of failure. I'd get the hell out but I won't ask Harry for the money. He'll ask for another … favor, in a long line of favors. And I'd rather die.

HOUSE RULES

A. Rey Pamatmat

Dramatic
Momo, early thirties. Filipino American

Momo is playing a Filipino board game with her sister, Twee. Momo, tired of Twee's incessant criticisms, snaps and lays into her.

MOMO

WHAT KIND OF SISTER ARE YOU! "You suck! This game sucks! Everything you do sucks! Your hair looks stupid! That outfit is stupid! YOU'RE STUPID!"

Well, you know what, Twee? YOU'RE STUPID! A STUPID PIECE OF CRAP! YES.

CRAAAAAAAP.

Maybe some of us are fine looking au naturel. Some of us don't measure our self-esteem by whether or not our hair bounces like Beyoncé's. Some of us don't need to look like high

fashion, call girl assassins who know how to put make up on so we don't look like clowns or triple-threat actor/singer/dancers in *Cats*. Because I HATE your shoes, your stupid slut heels! And I HATE that you call them slut heels! And I HATE when you tell me I need a pair! Because you're so mean! I don't want to look anything like a person who would be mean to her baby sister.

My friends' older sisters looked out for them and taught them how to pick nice clothes and whatever. But I got you. YOU! You mean, horrible piece of crap crap crap crap crap crap CRAP!!! YOU!!!

And maybe I don't want one of those smelly, farting, unshowered, unshaven jerks that your slut heels attract praying for this sinner now and at the hour of her death. AMEN.

AAAAAAAMEEEEEEEN—

THE JAG

Gino DiIorio

Seriocomic
Carla, thirty

Carla has Asberger's and has a tendency to talk to herself in Tourette's-like utterances. She is very intelligent, but lacking in social skills. She is speaking to "Chick," trying to reassure him that she does in fact know a great deal about repairing cars, and that she should let him repair his prize possession, a late model Jaguar sedan.

CARLA

No, no, gotta correct you there, Sir. Four mufflers. The fifth is called the resonator. So technically … *technically* … you could say five. But you'd be wrong!

(She laughs at her own joke again.)

Sorry. Four. And one resonator. Funny word, resonator. *Resonates.* Also, let's see … umm … .3 carburetors, very rare, very interesting system. One carb for two cylinders. Four universal joints, ooop—wait, wait, no fact in five. I mean, FIVE in fact. Independent Suspension in the rear and the front, all the way around, two fuel tanks, with a fuel pump for each, easy switch on the fly, sometimes a little tricky when it *rains* … the wiring, very difficult. Lucas wiring, the PRINCE OF DARKNESS! "Mister Lucas, what have you done?" A tangle of wires, like the roots of a tree. Such a *strange* wiring system. All stuffed in there. Underneath the dash, two finger turn bolts, take it off and you see all the fuses, with spare fuses sticking in, as if we're waiting for all this to blow! Now, whoever this *Lucas* was, *Mister* Lucas, I imagine a thin man, thick glasses, short cropped hair, who had a great *concept* as to how to wire an automobile—of course, we don't know if that's what he really looked like, and I don't want to know who he is … in fact, I never want to MEET the man, if you get my drift.

KILLING WOMEN

Marisa Wegrzyn

Seriocomic
Abby, thirties

Abby, a professional assassin, has been asked to speak to a classroom of kindergarten students on Career Day.

ABBY

Hi. My name is Abby. It's good to be here at Career Day. All your parents' jobs have sounded … fun. Especially Jonathan's dad who described working for twenty years at the same bank. You know the only job worse than that? My uncle used to masturbate turkeys for a living. Okay. Look. I'm not Tess's mom. Tess's mom now does my job. Or the job that I used to do. Yeah. Today was my first day off in a while. So I got up. Took a shower. Got dressed. I made toast. I burned it. This place smells like school. I hated school. Well I liked this one science class in high school. Our teacher, Mr. Gerard, wanted to prove that a body can only digest so much lactose—how many of you like lactose? Okay, nobody. How many of you like milk? Milk and lactose are the same thing. That was a trick question. Mr. Gerard, well he had all of us bring in a gallon of whole milk and a bucket, and we drank and drank until we threw up. In our buckets. You can try that at home. Mr. Gerard was a great teacher. He got fired for that class. But I learned a lot about the human digestive system that day. Here's my official Career Day advice. You're all going to grow up and get jobs, right? Some of you will hate your jobs, some of you won't really care, the lucky ones will like their jobs. You may get fired. No matter how good of a job you do, you might get fired for bullshit reasons … what, I can't say "shit"? Why the fuck not? … I can't say that either? All right. Shit. Sorry. I don't know. I been sitting here with all of you listening to all your parents with all their careers and I thought maybe coming in here today would give me some ideas, but it hasn't. Maybe you got some ideas. If you got some ideas, then that's good and this wasn't a big waste of time.

(takes out a paper)

I'm jumping to show and tell now. I got this fairy tale. Tess wrote it and her mom helped her with it. Tess did the pictures. Anyway, I like it. I don't know why. Some reason. The pictures are weird, but Tess is a weird kid. I'll just read some of this and call it a day, if that's okay. It's called *Princess Tess and the Moon Monsters*. "Once upon a time, there was a princess. She liked to run and jump rope and go to the pool in the summer. But more than anything, she liked to watch the moon change. Full to half to a teeny tiny sliver. But one night, it stopped changing. So the princess climbed on her rocket-ship, and blasted off to the moon because someone had to do something. And the princess could do anything. Anything at all. She could even fix the moon."

LAS CRUCES

Vincent Delaney

Dramatic
Jane, late forties

Jane makes a public statement about the horrific school shooting caused by her son Robbie. She's speaking to a crowd of reporters and hostile parents.

JANE

No, in answer to your question, we never had any warnings. Our son was seventeen, don't you think we'd notice? I'm sorry—could I just, I'd prefer to answer the questions as written, can we not—well, they're shouting at me, they're not supposed to, I agreed to answer these specific questions. We did not know about pipe bombs. I have never seen a pipe bomb. Wherever they were hidden, or how they were made, I just don't know, I DON'T KNOW. If you would ask them to respect this, this process, I agreed to answer these questions, my lawyer was clear, this is all I have to, just these questions. He must have bought the ammunition, I don't know, he worked at a pizza restaurant, that was his money, we didn't try to control—I never saw the guns. I never saw the bullets, or his journals. You don't snoop in your son's room, that's a violation of trust, do you understand? Have you considered that someone might have pressured him? I'm saying my son would not just go and buy bullets, there were probably all sorts of bad apples in the school, why are they shouting at me? Why are YOU SHOUTING AT ME? I can't think. You're not letting me think.

LAB RATS

Patrick Gabridge

Dramatic
Mika, mid-twenties to early thirties

Mika is talking to Jake, in the waiting room for a big sleep study. Jake didn't get in to the study, but he's there to wish Mika bon voyage. She's showed up carrying all her worldly possessions in a suitcase and a few trash bags.

MIKA

My roommates kicked me out. Complete bitches when it comes to paying the rent. I told them that once this experiment is done, I'll have plenty of cash. But Amanda is like, *you're three months behind,* and then Tiffany is all up in my grill about baking in the middle of the night, though I hardly ever complain when they're stomping around with their drunk ass boyfriends at one in the morning. And then one of them ate half the cupcakes that I'd baked, baked for you by the way. Last time, it cost me an entire catering gig. How am I supposed to pay my rent if they eat the fucking cupcakes that I'm supposed to sell to pay it? They laugh and act like it's a joke—me and my little bake sale life. But I stay, because the place is dirt cheap and has an actual kitchen. I hide out in my room and try not to mess with them. But she ate fucking my cupcakes. Amanda. I know it was her—little chocolate ring around the edges of her lips. Even so, maybe I should not have whacked her over the head with my cookie sheet. She's lucky I didn't have a fucking knife in my hand. She's pretty strong for a bulimic, spray-tanned little twat. I could have taken her if it wasn't for Tiffany jumping in. Two on one? How is that fair? And I'm the one who keeps the place clean, you know? Because I can't have their long, overly straightened, bleached blond hairs in my frosting. Who are they kidding? No one's hair is that straight. Look at this—they dented my bundt pan. How am I going to fix that? How am I going to fix any of it? Where am I going to go? This is it. All of my shit, in two bags and a suitcase. At least I've got a place to keep it all together for 73 days. But where am I going to stay until I get my check? I called to ask—do I get my check on the last day? Because I'm going to need it. And the lady on the phone, she says, *well, no, it usually takes four to six weeks to process the checks.* Complete fucking bullshit. But what can I do? I need to make it through the entire study first. Which I may or may not do. I might crack up from the isolation or boredom or from picking a fight with one of the other losers whose lives are so marginal they can spend two months sleeping with probes up their asses. My roommates already got the room rented out, to one of their little college friends. Stephanie. Tiffany, Amanda, and Stephanie. Jesus fucking Christ. I can't even go back there, because of the restraining order. More bullshit. Amanda's father is a lawyer—they whip that shit out like candy on Easter: *Here you go little girl, keep that bad roommate away. She's so scary.* I'm not the scary one. You should see the claws on that girl. She's had an entire army of Vietnamese manicurists applying polish for so long, they're like that guy from the X-men. Wolverine? I thought she was going to slice me to bits with those nails. Which is why I caught her upside the head with the cookie sheet. Which sounded good, but she wasn't hurt. It was all for show. *Big bad Mika, let's make sure she doesn't ever come back again. Throw all her shit out into the hall.* I come back and it's just one big pile. I had to borrow the bags from a neighbor. Anyway, I took what fit and left the rest. Let them deal with it. So that was my week. Fun times. How am I supposed to look for a new place when I'm in a hospital room day and night for the next two months? When I get out, I'm going to need a place to stay. A friend. I'm going to need a friend. So. You and me are friends. Right?

LIFE SUCKS
Aaron Posner

Dramatic
Pickles, forties

LIFE SUCKS is a hilarious loose adaptation of Chekhov's UNCLE VANYA. Pickles, a relentlessly positive utopian lesbian, bemoans an unrequited love.

PICKLES

Everyone is always saying to me—move on. "It's time to move on". That's the exact phrase that everyone uses, like some agreed upon plan: "It's time to Move On!" But here's the thing: I can't. I can't "move on". How can I? Because that love is still there. It still sits . . . right *there. [Pointing at her heart or gut or soul . . .].* I don't know how you all *[and she is talking simultaneously to the other actors and the audience ...]* can just go from one lover to another to another to another, I don't, not if that love is real. Not if it's *real.* Love is love and it stays forever. I think. I think it stays *forever.* I don't even know what people mean when they say "Oh, yeah, we really loved each other back then . . . " or "Yeah, I *used* to really love her" cause I just think: Where did that love go? *Where did that love go???* Because I don't know about you, but I still love everyone I've ever loved. Everyone I've ever loved, I still love. *[She starts crying right about here . . .]* And I think I always will. The truth is . . . I don't know how to stop. And . . . and the other truth is . . . I don't *want* to stop. My love for Iris is real. And I don't want to move on. I'm just fine where I am, thank you very much. I'm just fine right here . . .

LIFE SUCKS

Aaron Posner

Dramatic
Sonia, twenty-four

LIFE SUCKS is a hilarious loose adaptation of Chekhov's UNCLE VANYA. Here, Sonia tells Dr. Aster about her mother and her unrequited lust for a man.

SONIA

My mother used to say that our house was full of Radiant Invisible Butterflies. And every so often she'd call a hunt and a wild family excursion for Radiant Invisible Butterflies (or R.I.B.'s) would be on. I was really young, but I remember these episodes quite clearly. They were high points. But when I got older—I don't know, maybe 7 or 8, I finally asked her The Question. The Big One: Were they *real*? Were there *really* Radiant Invisible Butterflies fluttering around our house? Were there *really*? She told me they were just as real as I wanted them to be. She told me that the world was what *we made of it*. She told me that we had cause and effect all wrong, that we thought the world did things to us, and that *that* was the cause of our joy or suffering or *sadness* or whatever . . . But she said that that was totally wrong. *She said we were the cause.* She said we *choose* to be joyful or to suffer or to be sad . . . *and that we could always choose differently. That anything was possible.* If we could imagine . . . new possibilities. *[Beat . . .]* "Invisible *butterflies*"? *Where did that even come from?!?* I just told him some insane story about Radiant Invisible Butterflies when all I wanted to say was "please, please, please, take me upstairs right now, tear my stupid clothes off my stupid body with your teeth and fucking fuck me so hard and so well and so long that that that . . . that the bed breaks, and the universe disappears, and the sun stops in its rotation to see what all the fuss is about and the world comes crashing to a stop and our epic, ridiculous, sublime love-making is the last thing that the universe ever knows." But instead . . . I made up some story about invisible butterflies in a pathetic attempt to let him know I understand him and that he could do with me as he would . . . and I could see, totally clearly in his face that *he didn't get the message*. Not even close. It never even occurred to him because he cannot see me as a woman. Because the women that are real to him aren't like me . . .

LIFE SUCKS

Aaron Posner

Comic
Ella, thirty-six

*LIFE SUCKS is a hilarious adaptation of Chekhov's UNCLE VANYA. This
is direct address to the audience.*

ELLA

I like people, I really do. I find us all … *fascinating*. And *mysterious*.
And kind of irresistibly fucked up in such unique and broken little ways.
I genuinely want to know people and connect with them, I really do,
but … Can I ask you all a question? How many of you would like to
sleep with me if you could? I mean, hypothetically, if there were no
rules, no issues of *fidelity* or *morality* … or even *meta-theatricality* …
Just based on whatever it is you know about me right at this moment,
can we get a show of hands … ?

How many of you would just … pretty much like to have sex with
me? *[She counts, and then maybe comments ... or not ...]* Okay, fascinating. And now another question … How many of you are currently
just dying to sleep with someone other than the person you should
be sleeping with? Show of hands, please … *[Again she counts, and
then maybe comments ... or not ...]* Okay. Great. Now … You don't
have to raise your hands for this one, but … How many of you were
lying? Either because of who you are here with, or how you want to be
thought of in the world, or because of my feelings, or … Okay, here's
my point: As far as I can tell, we're all just in a twisty, impossible,
fucked up … yes, okay, *perdurable miasma* of "unmanageable urges"
vs. "moral imperatives", and instead of being able to just … *connect*
… just be in a kind and loving communion with our fellow human
beings, we're forever wrapped up in this … sexual *dance macabre* …
this *ridiculous relational gavotte* … this endless pursuit (and retreat)
of *unexpressed, unfulfilled, unexplored, unknowable needs* and *desires*
and *frustrations*.

LOUISE SPEAKS HER MIND

Martha Patterson

Seriocomic
Louise, thirties

Louise is the manager of a diner. She walks over to two women sitting at a table.

LOUISE

'Scuse me. Noticed you all talking. Those of us who work here got better things to do. But I do believe in good service. Sarah, here, she's our best. Hope you leave her a good tip. But I couldn't help overhearing you talk about men. Phooey!! … What makes you think they deserve your attention, anyway? Two pretty women, sitting in a diner, hashing it over about MEN? Don't you have better things to discuss? Like what to do about a woman's right to birth control when the Vatican's so opposed? Or the catastrophic problem of nuclear energy? Or our war on global warming? What are you thinking, anyway? Men are the be-all and end-all? Good Lord, I hope I have better sense than that. … Listen. I'm still young enough, but I got two kids already, and they're a handful. My mom takes care of them. And my kids' father left when I was only 25. But good riddance. He was a handful. And if I ever thought another man could be the answer, I hope some good person would bash me over the head with a glass bottle. Just smash it right over my head, to knock some sense into me. … Now, listen. When you get back to your office, don't dwell on how there's no good men. Don't ponder what could have been, if only you'd met Mr. Right. Don't fret. Instead, think about what fine jobs you have and how you're well able to take care of yourselves, and you can buy whatever you feel like, and pay your own rent, and don't you dare give a second thought to men. Waste of time. I should know. I support a family of three on my salary. And I'm the boss here at this restaurant. Top dog. And how do you think I did it? Education? No. A man? No. Hard work? You better believe it. We got more customers here than we can deal with. So many I'm thinking about getting rid of this place and moving up the road to somewhere twice the size. And Sarah here's like me. She works hard. *(Pause)* So you leave her a good tip, now, you hear?

THE LOVEBIRDS

Barbara Blumenthal-Ehrlich

Seriocomic
Marnie, thirties

Marnie is having an affair with Robert, a neighbor whom she met at the local supermarket, in the frozen foods section. Both are married, just not to each other. Here, she explains to him why she can't fall in love with him.

MARNIE

I can't fall in love with you! No. I mean, I *can't*. Like I can't speak French. Like I can't write with my left hand. I can't fall in love. I can't do it. Maybe it's like riding a bike or breathing to everybody else, but—I personally cannot fall in love. Not like 'til death do us part. Not even for an hour on Tuesday mornings. Love's crap. It's a blip, ok? A double rainbow … . a rare bird … . a four leaf clover. It's silent and fleeting and … . we try to tame it … domesticate it … . draaaaaaag it out. … have breakfast with it … . introduce it to our parents … have kids with it. But, Robert, the thing is: we're grabbing at steam. Before you know it, we mangle it. Destroy it. We fuck it up. Take it out on each other. End up dead inside. And that brings us right up to the present. I'm dead inside. I haven't felt my toes in years. The only reason things went so well for us was, one: you seemed happily married … and two: we were in "Frozen Foods." My temperature *inside* me matched the temperature *outside* in the store. If we had been in "Prepared Foods" none of this would have happened. I don't get hot. Not figuratively. Not literally. Nothing can warm me up. Not even soup. Not vegetable. Or lentil or … or … or … what the fuck, chicken matzoh ball. And it's not because anyone treated me badly or I was abused or felt unwanted. And it's not because I don't wish I could. I wish I could. Desperately. It's just not in my DNA. I'm a freak of nature. Or maybe just a straight up freak. I'd love to know what all the fuss is about. Not just 'cause it looks awesome in the movies. Or, because people will practically walk on hot coals—lie, cheat, steal and even kill—for it. But because … well, frankly … I'm lonely. The more is not the merrier. In fact, I feel worse and worse and worse every time one of these things fails.

After you, Robert, I swear, it's a straight drop. God, saying that out loud … just … feels … great. You wanna fuck or not?

For information on this author, click on the WRITERS tab at www.smithandkraus.com.

LULLABY

Michael Elyanow

Dramatic
Thea, late forties

*Thea—who's always had a hard time opening up—confesses to her friend
Cassie about the dark depression she fell in after her girlfriend's betrayal.*

THEA

The day of the surgery, when Shannon called me to say she was stuck
in traffic, she told me to take a cab to the hospital. Promised she'd be
there before they operate. She wasn't. Operation comes, no call from
her. Nothing. I remember thinking, just before I went under, we've been
together for so long, she wouldn't do this to me. She'll be here when
I come out. She wasn't. That night, lying in that hospital bed, alone,
no calls answered, no messages for me, I'm staring up at the cork-
board ceiling honest to God thinking: did I make it? Am I alive? Cuz I
don't understand. I mean, the only thing that could explain her choosing
fear, over me, is that I must be dead—only death makes more sense. .
.. You don't know, Cassie, you don't know until they take away your
body parts what else gets taken from you. The one person I counted
on, the only one I trusted ... removed herself. *(beat)* Cassie, I can't
handle another rough patch. I won't make it through. I won't.

MARIE AND ROSETTA

George Brant

Dramatic
Rosetta, thirties, African American

Sister Rosetta Tharpe, a famous gospel singer and guitar player who basically created Rock and Roll, is talking to Marie Knight, a talented young singer she has hired to perform with her. They are in the casket room of a funeral home in the deep South, preparing for a gig that night. This is where they will sleep.

ROSETTA

Honey, maybe you noticed we ain't playin' no Carnegie Hall tonight. No Savoy Ballroom. No Café Society. We playin' in a warehouse. Tobacco warehouse on the outskirts of town. Dresses gonna stink of smoke for a week. Next night's a barn, after that a hangar. Anywhere a bunch a black folk congregatin' won't be noticed. There's rules down here We northern Negroes, we got to be invisible. We step off stage and we got to disappear. Beds? Down here we depend on the Good Samaritan Circuit for a bed, cuz God knows there ain't no room at the inn. Sometimes it's somebody's garage, kitchen, couch; and sometimes it's a miracle like this. A piano in the corner, plenty a' elbow space and a showroom to choose from for when we lay down our heads. Your choice. Cot or casket. I'm a casket gal myself. Like sleeping on a cloud. Well you keep an eye out for ghosts I'm gonna be snoring in the corner, in the deluxe satin-lined model. And you thank Walter in the morning you hear? Whether you sleep all night or just a minute cuz'a ghostwatchin' you thank him. Good Samaritan Walter of "Walter's Funeral Home and InsuranceCompany." Cuz without him little Marie would be sleeping the night inthe bus cute little black girl out there sleeping under her coat pretty face in the window for all the white world to see. Someday I'll get enough money, deck that bus out put some beds in there. Mirrors, closets, dressing, rooms. Won't have to worry 'bout this every night. Until then we depend on our friends Wherever we find them. Understood?

MARIE AND ROSETTA

George Brant

Dramatic
Rosetta, thirties, African American

Sister Rosetta Tharpe, a famous gospel singer and guitarist who basically created what came to be known as Rock and Roll, is admonishing Marie Knight, a young woman who has recently hired to perform with her, not to sell herself short.

ROSETTA

Don't lie to me girl. We can't build this up on no lyin' foundation. You tell the truth or we over before we start. Who's better on piano? Huh? That's right you. You better. You own up to your gifts girl. You got to know what they worth, truly worth, or you got nothing. My Mother Bell taught me that. I was little girl eight or so. Mother Bell and I come out to sing middle of the service. Black folk in front of me smiling and praising. And then I look up, see all them white folk in the balcony, Up in the Heaven section. The ones who showed up every Sunday for a little entertainment, come to see the holy rollers in action. And then I hear it. A distant sound. A jingle jangle in pockets. I see a glint of something and feel a sting on my cheek. And then the shower proper starts. The copper shower from the balcony. Pennies from Heaven. And some of the black folk are scrambling to pick 'em up but I know Mother Bell told me not to lower myself, not to be one of those scramblers, but my cheek stings it was kissed by one of them and I know what a penny buys just one how much candy that one penny buys and I see it at my feet it's there at my feet and I slidle my right foot over and cover that copper. I'm thinking I'll save that one just that one and we finish and the clapping brings more copper but I don't pick them up. I don't stoop. I just shuffle. I just shuffle-walk that penny back to the pew with my Mother Bell at my side and I'm thinkin' I finally outsmarted her for once, but the minute we sit down she whacks that right leg of mine with her cane. She didn't fall for my jake walk after all and now what do I got? I got the eight year-old blues: A big ugly bruise on my leg and no penny to show for it. I was mad but Mother Bell was right. Even then, even at eight years old I was worth more than a white man's pocket change. You got to know. You got to know what your gift's worth.

MARIE AND ROSETTA

George Brant

Dramatic
Rosetta, thirties, African American

Sister Rosetta Tharpe, and famous gospel singer and guitarist whose style foreshadowed Rock and Roll is rehearsing with Marie Knight, a sweet young thing she has hired to perform with her. They have been singing "Rock Me in the Cradle of Our Love" but Marie is dissatisfied with the way Marie is singing it.

ROSETTA

No! No no no no no! Who are *you*? Some 17 year-old 23 year-old come in here and think you can … No. RRRRRRROCK ME! RRRRRRROCK ME! That's what the people down here come to see .That's what they travel on a wagon ten miles to see. What they saved up for. What they dress up for. They come to hear that RRRRRROCK ME for theyselves. I am bringing them joy with that Rock Me you hear? Joy. So no I ain't changin' that. And if you gonna be lookin over my shoulder every second of every day then we can forget this whole thing right now. Why don't we do that, why don't you stay here with your ghosts

and I will rock that warehouse to the ground and tomorrow you can take your skinny ass —

(to Marie)

Pardon

(to Heaven)

Pardon - back home. And as for your soul, Your precious pure two-baby soul, I'll take care of it as best I can but that's a personal thing. That's between you and the Lord. That's up to you Me, I know I'm right with Him. You gotta fend for yourself

MIMESOPHOBIA

Carlos Murillo

Dramatic
Shawn, thirties

Shawn, a high strung academic, finds herself on the verge of a nervous breakdown as she tries to complete a tome on violent televised entertainment. In an attempt to complete her book, she goes off to a writers retreat in southern California where she spirals out of control. In this scene, she reaches out by writing a postcard to her long estranged mother who she blames for her mental instability.

SHAWN

The city dweller imagines her surroundings as permanent - something that has been for a long time and will be for a long time, long after the city dweller's relocation to the necropolis. This sense of permanence is one among the billion white lies the city dweller must tell herself in order to go on with "business as usual," in order to function as a normal, productive human being. But in this city that lie is no more protective than a T-shirt on an Arctic glacier. The whole subtext of this place is impermanence and impending doom. Despite the eternal sunshine, every city dweller here knows that beneath the surface lurks a slumbering dragon, which, once woken, will swallow the city, landscape, citizenry in one abysmal gulp. I take comfort knowing that here, death could strike any minute. Apocalypse is no further away than a tick of the clock. Cataclysm loiters on every street corner. I soak in the generosity of the sun, shining as consolation for the perpetually present end.

For information on this author, click on the WRITERS tab at
www.smithandkraus.com.

MORNING AFTER GRACE

Carey Crim

Seriocomic
Abigail, sixty-two

Abigail, a widow, has recently joined an online dating service. She tells Angus, a retired lawyer whom she has picked up at his wife's funeral, what that's like.

ABIGAIL

Did you know that by age fifty, the number of single men to women is about equal, but by sixty, it's a little more than two women for every one man. By seventy, it's four to one. My coach had me make this video for my profile. Though I honestly don't know when you guys have time to even glance at a video because, according to all of *your* profiles, you're out taking long walks on the beach, hiking Kilimanjaro and then jetting home to cook organic, locally sourced farm to table dinners. Anyway, she made me redo it like nine times. I wasn't coming across as low-maintenance enough. She said I had to be fun, flirty and warm. Nurturing, but not overwhelming. Receptive, but not too easy to catch or else I'll repel the illusive alpha male who is, who are we kidding, probably out banging his thirty-five year old yoga instructor anyway. It's so strange to feel invisible. I don't know when that happened. One day you're walking down the street, getting annoyed by the cat calls, and it seems like the very next day those same men are calling you ma'am and just two days after that, some good looking guy is offering you his seat on the bus. And it's not because he thinks you're pretty or, I don't know, even pregnant. It's because he thinks you are too old to hold yourself upright. I may pee a little when I sneeze but I can still stand up!

For information on this author, click on the WRITERS tab at
www.smithandkraus.com.

THE MOVING OF LILLA BARTON

John MacNicholas

Dramatic
Lilla, fifties - sixties

Lilla's only husband, Edward Barton, was the beloved rector of this church for more than two decades before he died unexpectedly of a massive heart attack. A year later, Lilla has stubbornly refused to move out of the rectory, even though the new priest has now been appointed. Her grief and anguish have put her in conflict not only with the parish, for which she has done remarkable service, but also with God. This prayer occurs late in the play, after we have witnessed Lilla fighting a pitched battle against depression and despair.

LILLA

God from God, Light from Light, true God from true God, begotten, not made—God from God, Light from Li —

(Tone changes; paraphrasing a Psalm.)

Oh, my remorseless God! I cry in the daytime and at night, but who hears? How long will You hide your face from me? . . .The long shadows have settled here and do not leave. If I knew what death is I might know life—feel it again as once I did before Edward left. How those eyes of his—blue as hydrangeas—scattered such joy, planting it everywhere. Oh, when he and I were married, the priest was confused, more jittery than we were saying the vows, and he blurted "I now pronounce you man and life." Edward never forgot that. Man and life . . .Eyes blue as hydrangeas even when they lost their brightness—slowly, then quickly, how they lost that shining expectancy. If I could only forget! . . .His voice came to me in bed last night, clear as clear could be, and he asked for a glass of water. I arose and got it. When I leaned over to give him the water he was not there. Not there, even though I could still smell him next to my pillow. That's all death seems, a perverse refusal to come back. Well, how am I to live on this earth? If only You would give me sleep, I might abide the intolerable agony of Edward being not here, never here, never ever again eyes blue as hydrangeas . . .Do not let my heart shrivel in silence in this room where I have loved and been loved. Oh, my God of light, Destroyer—and Preserver—I beg You, grant me asylum from my own memory!

For information on this author, click on the WRITERS tab at www.smithandkraus.com.

MY LIFE AS YOU

Laura Rohrman

Dramatic
Diana, twenty-three

Diana has been letting her friend Stella stay with her for the past month in her apartment in Chicago. Stella ran away from her life in San Francisco and has been depressed. She says she wants to be a reporter, but all she's been doing is lying around pining away for ex-boyfriend who still lives in San Francisco. Diana is type A, and can get a job as a reporter as a side job, while still having a regular job. Diana is ruled by competition about everything—jobs and boyfriends included.

DIANA

I am not the one making YOU miserable, Stella. A little competition never hurt anyone—don't you agree? Writer, writer . . . oh you think you're a writer. You never even applied for the jobs. You just talked about it. I do things, Stella. I get more done than most people—and it's because I'm worried. I don't want to be 30 and have done nothing with my twenties. You are the most indolent—oh Stella, a little competition will be good for you. You like to live off of IDEAS. I did this, I traveled here or there . . . What have you done lately, Stella? Do you ever ask yourself that? Have you ever noticed that this way you are—this depression thing that you are going through—have you ever thought for a minute about how you are affecting those around you? Did you ever think that your self-serving behavior is making me miserable? I worry every day . . . just look at the way that you lay around this place.

(Paces around nervously.)

I even worry that you might kill yourself. If you want to do something then do it. I don't know if you are a good writer or not, but I know that I am . . . I can't make Chicago a happy place for you. I can't make your life happy. I'm not going to not apply for jobs just because somebody won't get off her ass and apply for them herself. You need some competition, Stella. You need someone to push you.

For information on this author, click on the WRITERS tab at
www.smithandkraus.com.

ONEGIN AND TATYANA IN ODESSA

Don Nigro

Dramatic
Tatyana, thirties

St. Petersburg, Russia, in the 1820s. Tatyana is confronting Onegin, a man she once offered herself to when she was a teenage girl in the country. Then, Onegin, older, more experienced, and a bit of a scoundrel, had chosen not to take advantage of her and gently rejected her advances. Later, Onegin killed his friend Lensky in a duel over Onegin's attentions to Lensky's beloved, her sister, and Tatyana was married off to a rich older man. Now, some years after, Onegin has returned to St Petersburg and discovered Tatyana all grown up and a Princess, and has fallen hopelessly in love with her. She has kept her distance, but the distraught Onegin has come to her home and begged her to give him another chance. He's been very uncharacteristically sobbing with his head in her lap. Here she finds herself in the difficult position of rejecting a man she still loves because she's now married to a man she doesn't.

TATYANA

Just shut up and listen to me a moment. I suppose you deserve some sort of explanation, at least. Do you remember when we met in the garden, and you gave me a sermon about life? Well, now it's my turn. I was very, very young. And I loved you. It was foolish, but I loved you with all my heart. And what did I find in yours? Nothing. Instead you gave me a cynical, self-dramatizing lecture about how good it was of you not to take advantage of me. But I don't accuse you. I suppose you might say it actually was a noble thing you did, throwing the little fish back. In fact, I'm grateful. In a way. But then, what are you doing now? Of all the people in the world to choose from, why me? Because I'm rich now, and married to a Prince? Are you sure you don't just want to stain my reputation in order to enhance yours as a seducer? I'm crying. It's foolish. I'd have preferred that you'd been openly cruel to me, instead of giving me that lecture. But you at least had some dignity. Now look at you. What's happened to you? To make yourself a slave to such a trivial emotion. Do you really think any of this matters to me? Money and position and all of that. None of it matters. I'd give it all up to be back there, in the garden. We come so close and then we fail, somehow, to connect. Perhaps I was wrong to marry someone I couldn't love. But my mother wanted it so badly. How could I refuse her this one thing, when it meant so little to me? What difference did it make who I married, after what happened? You need to go now. I know you're not as bad as you seem. There is something good in you. And I do love you. But I've been given to somebody else, and if there's one thing I learned from you, it's that the worst thing is betrayal. There is nothing worse. My husband has many faults. But I believe he does love me, in his way, and he has chosen me, and put his trust in me. And I will never betray him. Never. Don't say anything more to me. Just go.

OTHER THAN HONORABLE

Jamie Pachino

Dramatic
Grace Rattigan, early thirties

Grace Rattigan, a former Army officer who resigned under sealed terms, is now an attorney. Grace was a victim of a military sexual assault from a man who is now a Brigadier General about to be appointed Deputy Inspector General of the Army. Grace has scrupulously avoided any military cases in her practice, but reluctantly takes on the case of a PFC who was assaulted on her same base as the play begins. In this moment, Grace raises the stakes of her case to include the Brigadier General and his base in her suit.

GRACE

I'm suing the base. I'm filing a countersuit on behalf of my client against the conditions that led to her getting continually sexually assaulted then raped under the watchful eye of Commander Gideon Kane. I'm suing the base, the First Sergeant, the army, and your precious Commander because he was the CO for the years leading up to this incident. He trained the officers who carried out his policy, and *he set the tone.* So I will question a command whose climate led to cruel and inhumane treatment getting rewarded with promotions, and victims treated with retaliation. My God, if we heard about these assaults happening in any other country, we'd *invade them.* I know the military's about wiping out individuality—but there are people inside those uniforms who put their lives in jeopardy every day to defend us and we're failing them. You say things have changed, but what? Jesus Hector, in the eight years since I walked away, what the hell has changed? After everything done to this 22 year old woman, she's the one called Other Than Honorable? Can't we do better than that?

For information on this author, click on the WRITERS tab at
www.smithandkraus.com.

PERILOUS NIGHT

Lee Blessing

Dramatic
Harriet, mid to late twenties, African American

Harriet is in a mental-health facility. She has escaped from her wing and is now in the wing (and room) of another patient, an older white woman who thinks she's Queen Elizabeth III of England. This is the first time they've met, and this is more or less the first thing Harriet tells her.

HARRIET

One night, I met a man—way, way out in one of the wings—far from where they have me. This man was much, much older than me—or even you. Little white hairs were sprouting on him. He was a black man, and frail—and almost totally bald too, except for these little, straggly hairs. They came out his ears and upper arms and cheeks and even his eyelids. Have you ever seen that? Someone so old their hairs just show up any old place? Am I talking too much? I don't mean to be. I can leave. *(no response)* I forget where he was. It was a wing off another wing. He was blind. That old man? The one with the hairy eyes? He thought I was his daughter Verna—called me by her name and everything. I even pretended I was Verna. Turned out she'd been dead for forty years, so I just filled him in on what she'd been doing since the funeral. I told him she—or I said "I"—said I'd mostly been at Disneyland, but that I made sure to improve myself and travel a lot too. And the travel was free of course, since I was dead. I saw the Taj Mahal, that big Buddha in Japan and the Great Rift Valley in Africa. He loved it so much. I was his only visitor. Everyone he knew was dead—he was so old, see. To make him feel better I started playing his wife and his great-grandson and his old boss and he *really* loved that, and we went on and on that way right through the night. *(beat)* At the end I went back to being Verna again, 'cause she was the one he loved most. I told him how much I thought about him when I was on the Great Wall of China or riding Space Mountain. Then I kissed him on the forehead and said goodnight. Then he laughed a wheezy kind of laugh and said, "There ain't no Verna. I ain't never had no daughter in my life." Then he laughed *real* hard, and then he died. *(after a beat, suddenly realizing)* Sometimes I think I just dreamed him.

PLANCHETTE

Carolyn Gage

Dramatic
Jude, teens

Jude is a rather masculine looking girl. She is talking to another girl, Mollie. Both girls have been sharing their secrets about trauma they have survived and the deeper secrets about their sexual orientations and gender identities. Mollie's father, a minister, has just shamed her for wearing men's clothing and doing "men's work," explaining how it is the responsibility of men to take care of women.

JUDE

(exploding in fury)

Men taking care of women? My pa went off to Denver and left us in that ... *shack!* ... For weeks—sometimes a whole month! Just me and my mother ... And if it hadn't been for me bucking wood and doing all the cooking, we would have frozen and starved to death! She couldn't do *anything* ... just sit there and talk to herself and cry all day. And then she tried to burn down the house ... *nine times!*

(sobbing and nearly incoherent)

She tried to burn it down *nine times ... with us in it!* I couldn't let her alone for a minute ... I had to stay up at night, watching her ... What was I supposed to do? Tie my mother up like an animal ... ? *What was I supposed to do?* But sometimes I just couldn't keep awake, no matter how much coffee I drank. So one night last summer, I fell asleep and she did it. She lit a fire in every room. When I woke up, the whole house was on fire, and there she was ... standing there in her nightgown, laughing. If it hadn't been for me, she would have burned up! She didn't care. She didn't care if I died, either. She was just standing there laughing. Wouldn't even help me pump water, when I was running back and forth, working my legs off trying to put it out ... By morning, it was all burned up. Everything we owned. Burned to cinders ... And then folks said it was my fault. They said I should have done something. What was I supposed to do? *What the hell was I supposed to do?*

PLUCKER

Alena Smith

Seriocomic
Thomasina, late twenties

Wealthy, beautiful Thomasina tells her friend Alexis how happy she is to be engaged to Julian, who was Alexis's best friend in college. Alexis listens, envious.

THOMASINA

You know what's crazy? We've been doing it even more since we got engaged. All I have to do is think about how I felt when Julian proposed . . . and it's like - do me. Now. It was so beautiful, Lexie. That moment. It was our last day on the Vineyard - we'd been at the beach all day. And you know that feeling you have when you've been at the beach for hours and hours - like your skin has absorbed the heat of the sun - and your mind has absorbed the crash of the waves - and you're completely relaxed - you're like, *part of the beach* - and the air is salty and fresh - and it's beginning to cool off into the evening . . . I was lying on my side, turned away from Julian, and there was this little girl. She was such a pretty little girl, in a blue striped suit, and I was staring at her, and all of a sudden I slipped into a dream. I was dreaming that she was my baby, our baby, and if I rolled over, Julian would be there, but he'd be older, and I'd be older, and we'd have this little girl. And then I felt Julian's hand on my back, and I turned to face him, and looked into his eyes, and he was crying. And that's when he asked me to marry him.

For information on this author, click on the WRITERS tab at
www.smithandkraus.com.

PLUCKER

Alena Smith

Dramatic
Alexis, late twenties

Alexis confronts her best friend Julian about his decision to marry Thomasina.

ALEXIS

It's no wonder I scare you. Honestly? Julian - you're kind of a wimp. Look - I know you're in love with her. But I need to say this. I need to say it to you now so I don't have to stand up at your wedding and say it in front of everyone. I think you gave up on yourself when you met Thomasina. And I think she let you give up. There are things about you - important things - that Thomasina is never going to accept. And you've let her pick and choose. It's like she got to pluck out the parts of Julian she likes, and throw away the parts of Julian she doesn't like. You used to be made up of all these parts - and now you're - simpler. You let her simplify you. But I miss the old Julian. I miss the complicated Julian - the one who wasn't toned down, airbrushed, streamlined - the one who wasn't so fucking *happy all the time!*

For information on this author, click on the WRITERS tab at
www.smithandkraus.com.

PLUCKER

Alena Smith

Seriocomic
Lee, twenty-nine

_Lee, a dancer, is having an emotional breakdown. Here, she tells her
friend Alexis why._

LEE

I was crying because - I'm a loser! I'm almost thirty years old. I'm
broke. My fifth metatarsal's all fucked up. I can't afford to go to
the doctor. I can't afford to even _think_ about having a baby! I can't even
sleep in my bed tonight because the very religious Mexican family I
live with found my freaking _vibrator_ in their bathroom, Yeah, I get
awoken from my alcoholic coma at four P.M. today by Senora Sanchez
banging open my door, eyes covered, screaming "_Los muchachos!
Mira_! They see! _Todo el mundo_! The children! The children!" And
she's waving my _purple fucking dildo_ in the air. Her kids found it in
the bathroom. I left it there. BECAUSE I WAS DRUNK!!! So now
I need to find a whole new living situation. I'm a loser, Alexis. In
the eyes of Senora Sanchez, in the eyes of the world. I'm a pathetic,
broke-ass, fucked-up lesbian _vagabond_ - and the worst part is - the
worst part is - _(Slight pause.)_ How do I even know that I'm gay? My
girlfriend says - if I could fall in love with a guy - then I probably
will, again. But what if it was just - _him_? You know? What if _he_ was
the one? You know - what if I found him again? Maybe - shit! I don't
know! Half of me just wants to go back in time and be twenty years
old again. But the other half is like, _no._ You're an adult! I just want to
be an adult - like, with _money._ And a _wife._ Or - husband. Whatever.
Dude, I don't know. _How do people do it?!_ Why can't I figure it out?
I just want what you have, Alexis!

For information on this author, click on the WRITERS tab at
www.smithandkraus.com.

PLUCKER

Alena Smith

Dramatic
Alexis, late twenties

Alexis, who just moved in with her boyfriend and isn't sure it was the right decision, laments her single days.

ALEXIS

Sometimes I just wish I was single. I just want to go to a party by myself again. You know? I want to have a crush on someone again! You know how it is - when you set your sights on someone. Maybe it's at a show, maybe he's playing guitar, and looking dark and melancholy, and you say to yourself - that's him, he's it, and I am going to get with him. Tonight. And even though the room is full of other perfectly attractive women who might be thinking the exact same thing, at this precise moment you kind of light up, and you know you have it in you to make it happen. Tonight. You know that strange, cosmic needles are weaving you and him together with burning threads of fire. You know that he will be unable to resist you. And it's true. You stick it out till three in the morning, drinking and smoking way too many cigarettes, talking to other guys you're not the slightest bit attracted to, watching him flirt with other girls, but always catching your eye at the last possible second before you were about to give up, letting you know with one hot glance that it's on, he just has to get rid of this one and then he'll make his way over to you. And then he does, he makes his way over to you, and he puts his hand on the small of your back, and you feel calm, safe, protected, even though you are going up in flames. And this is what you give up when you settle down. You give up this crazy magic that it took you years to perfect. It's like an arrow-maker having to put down his tools and stop making arrows. No more setting your sights on someone. No more sending fiery arrows zooming through the dark. *(Beat.)* I just want to meet someone again who sets me on fire.

For information on this author, click on the WRITERS tab at
www.smithandkraus.com.

POPCORN AT THE ODESSA

Don Nigro

Seriocomic
Becky, twenty-two

By the late autumn of 1949 Becky, twenty-two, a troubled young woman whose mother Jessie died when Becky was born and has never been certain who her father was, has already given birth to two daughters as a teenager, to a sinister carnival man, and her first husband has hung himself in the barn. She is now married to Johnny Palestrina, war hero son of Italian immigrants, and has not long ago given birth to her third child, Ben. John is good to her and she now has a nice house and a stable life, but she finds herself incapable of enjoying it. Part of her feels trapped, afraid of her children, and uneasy about herself and her life. She loves Johnny but is not happy and spends most of her days rearranging the furniture in the house. Here they sit out in the back yard on an Indian Summer night in November and she tries to explain to him why she is unhappy.

BECKY

How can I trust you if you act like you love me? And don't tell me you do love me, because I've heard that bullshit before. I don't believe it. And if I did believe it, you'd bore the hell out of me and I'd want to be someplace else with somebody who treated me like crap. I'm a mess. What if our baby turns out like me and not you? I mean, June and Lorry are nothing like me. Well, June's nothing like me. Lorry is nervous and high strung like me but that's all. She's so smart it's terrifying. What if Ben grows up like me and not like you? I don't know. There's still moths around. Why are there still moths around? All the moths are supposed to be dead now. You can't trust those bastards. No matter what you do, they eat everything. God sends them. He sends the moths to eat everything we love. Then he makes us buy moth balls, but moth balls are poison. We can't have moth balls because the baby will eat them and die. So there's moths everywhere, and they eat the baby. Okay. That's stupid. I know that's stupid. I'm stupid. I don't understand the rules of Canasta. Everybody tries to teach me but it just doesn't make any sense to me. How can I be expected to take care of children when I can't even learn to play Canasta? Why did you even want me? Because I'm pretty? Because I've got a message for you, buddy: I'm not always going to be pretty. Aunt Moll used to be pretty. All the boys were after her. And look at her now. She's stuck with Uncle Clete. How attractive can she be if she's stuck with Uncle Clete? If you think my Aunt Moll is so damned attractive then maybe you should marry her and leave me alone. My mother was pretty. And look what it got her: pregnant and dead. I live in fear. I'm constantly afraid. Every second. Children make my skin crawl. They're not human. And when you're around children, anything you say or do can be like this enormously important thing to them, and you don't even know it. You forget it the next second but they remember for the rest of their lives. Children scar so easily. Everything stands for something with them. The whole world is like a fairy tale and you're the ogre. I don't know what I'm saying. I don't know what I want. I don't know what to do. So I just keep rearranging the furniture all day in the hope that somehow, if I just manage to find the right configuration, everything will finally make some sort of sense. *(Pause)* Do you know why I married you? Because I thought you were dangerous. I mean, you went to France and killed people with a bazooka and you're Italian, for God's sake. I come from good honest Protestant farm people with blue eyes and freckles. Everybody knows Italians are all a bunch of violent, dangerous criminals. We saw it at the movies. But you tricked me. You're not like that. You're nice. You're funny, and kind, and patient, and strong, and you're good to my kids, who hate me and absolutely worship you. People like you scare the living hell out of me.

THE POWER OF DUFF

Stephen Belber

Dramatic
Sue, thirty-four

Sue Raspell, the uptight and fastidious co-anchor of a TV news broadcast comes to her co-anchor Charlie Duff's dressing room and reveals a different side to her, namely that her marriage is loveless and she wants to leave her husband.

SUE

We have different ways of dealing with our son. We didn't at first. Then we did. So that's how it started. *(pause)* And now we barely communicate, we sleep in separate rooms, we haven't *touched* each other in . . . .what feels like years.

(She is standing very still, eyes perhaps closed.)

You try so hard to make things work. You do a million things you don't want to. You smile when you wanna cry; you tidy up when you want to . . . wreak havoc. I make eighty per cent of the money, I do ninety per cent of the work around the house, I care for our child, I try to be a loving person and then my husband tells me I have a pole up my ass. It's not . . . how I was meant to live.

(maybe opening her eyes)

I used to be a loving person, Charles. I used to be fucking care-free, I swear to God. I used to have . . . wanderlust; I used to collect bugs; I used to make sweet potato pancakes; I used to want to take flying lessons; I used to listen to a hundred different types of music; I used to fix everything that was broken in the house; I used to cut my own hair; I used to take my son to the park every Saturday to play with his boat in the pond. And now I look at myself . . . and I'm a stranger. I'm a shell. I don't like drinking my coffee in the morning anymore, I don't hum in the shower, I don't buy interesting underwear, I don't bake people birthday cakes, I don't dance, I don't enjoy my job, I don't like my husband, I don't kiss my son enough, I don't . . . *(near whisper)* I don't know what I'm doing.

For information on this author, click on the WRITERS tab at
www.smithandkraus.com.

PROMISING

Michelle Elliott

Dramatic
Verity, forty

Verity is serving as the Campaign Manager for a promising up-and-coming politician in New York City. She is extremely driven and committed to helping David succeed, in large part because she has a strong emotional attachment to him.

VERITY

If David gets this seat, he's a shoe-in to become Speaker, which is like being the Mayor's right hand. Two years from now when the current Mayor term limits out, who do you think will be the favorite to take his spot? Being the Mayor of New York is a national platform, way better than being Governor of about 30 of the shittier states. Once David's Mayor, he'll be poised for national office, not the bullshit House, but something with actual meat, like Senate or a cabinet post, a good one, not Health and Human Services. Small step from there to being a potential VP candidate, and after that, the party'll beg him to take a crack at the White House, so, that's the big deal. This isn't about me, it's about David. Your brother is one of the most promising young politicians in the country. All he has to do is get through the next 13 days without anyone, unemployed, trouble-making little sisters included, coming along to fuck it up and then everything he's been working for is his for the taking. Activists are the people who get in the way of those who are actually trying to get something done. Your brother is going to be in a position to actually change policy and make the world a better place, but a whiff of scandal makes him vulnerable. Wouldn't you regret it if you were the cause of him not being elected? If you fuck this up for him there'll be one less voice in the world that can actually get something done.

PROMISING

Michelle Elliott

Dramatic
Gemma, twenty

Gemma Carver woman who grew up in Hong Kong. Her mother was Chinese and her father, who was an American Ambassador to China, was Caucasian. She is now studying environmental sciences in the U.S. and is a deeply-committed environmental activist.

GEMMA

Don't feel bad, it's all gonna be over soon. Life as we know it. Possibly all life on the planet. We've got about 13 years left. According to scientists. You're smart. Look at the data on climate change, deforestation, human sprawl, rising sea levels, glacier melt rates and whatever you come up with, multiply it by greed and apathy. We're basically fucked. A way for us to fix it all? Yeah, that's what everyone assumes. That when things get really bad there will be some sort of global effort to reverse climate change. But do you really think we can really whip that up in a few months? Especially when we're defunding every project that could have even a tiny positive impact on the environment, not to mention thwarting the validity of science on a daily basis. Sometimes I get so stressed out about it I feel like my head is gonna burst. The only thing that calms me down is knowing that when the planet does explode in the most enormous fireball ever . . . so will all the assholes who fucked it up so badly. And to me, that's poetry.

PROMISING

Michelle Elliott

Dramatic
Verity, forty

Verity Jones is serving as the Campaign Manager for a promising up-and-coming politician in New York City. She is in love with him and has been for some time, but he doesn't return her feelings. He has just told Verity that he slept with a young woman he met in a bar, which devastates her.

VERITY

I thought you just didn't have time for something real. That you didn't want to deal with any distractions, so I took what crusts I could get. A few precious nights when you were too tired to think of a reason why not or too busy to find a woman you actually wanted. But I guess you wanted the girl. Why her? Why not me? If it was just sex you needed, why not me? Don't respect me. I'd be fine with that. I'd be fine with you not respecting me. I'm here and willing … Men desire whores. Men lust after whores. You've never wanted me, but here I am, unable to draw a fucking breath without thinking of you. Every phone call, every grubby dollar raised, every shaken hand, deal made, vote promised, arm twisted, was a question, a beg, really, me begging you to just fucking love me, please. There'll be no one more devoted, more attuned, more practiced at meeting your every need, committed to making you happier than happy—blissful. So loved. So beautiful and wanted, there could be no reason to want or need anything again. That's how I would love you. You're carved out of me, do you know what I mean? Like a spoon hollows out an avocado. Shitty metaphor but I'm not a poet, I'm just an idiot who believed in the wrong man.

PROMISING

Michelle Elliott

Dramatic
Gemma, twenty

Gemma Carver grew up in Hong Kong. Her mother was Chinese and her father, who was an American Ambassador to China, was Caucasian. She is now studying environmental sciences in the U.S. and is a deeply-committed environmental activist.

GEMMA

Poop bags are disgusting. But think about this when you're picking up the pile of shit. You're picking it up with a plastic bag and then you tie it off and throw it away. Imagine what it will be like 1,000 years from when it starts to disintegrate and the first wave of poop bags and disposable diapers finally corrode enough for the toxic stew inside to start seeping out. I know it's disgusting but life is disgusting and looking away won't help anything. I mean, think about childbirth, not for the squeamish, and death is no better, much worse, actually. You could die in a horrible accident, like falling into an industrial gum mixing machine, don't laugh, it's happened to real people, or from a terrible disease (and I could list some if you want me to) ... or if you're super lucky, you die in your sleep surrounded by whatever assemblage of assholes you've managed to string along ... but you're still headed for the mortician's slab, you're still gonna be dripping out onto some steel table, your run-off, what was previously your life force, running into a drain, sluicing with juices of hundreds before you. And that is disgusting, but it's also kind of beautiful, depending on your definition of beautiful.

SISTER SISTER

Barbara Blumenthal-Ehrlich

Dramatic
Dirdra, thirties

Dirdra is speaking to her estranged sister, Janice. Dirdra ran away in her teens, leaving Janice alone with their crazy mother. They've been reunited for the mother's funeral, happy that she's finally dead. Here, Dirdra explains why she can't participate in a memorial service and how she'd have maternal fantasies about a customer at the supermarket deli counter, taking care of her children. When she first learned of her mother's death, Dirdra got confused, the fantasy became reality and she wept for the woman at the deli counter.

DIRDRA

Hey! I'm here now, and I know what's what and who's dead, and I'm completely sane and happy. Happy and sane. So just drop it. *You* do this. Don't act like it's so … . You do it. You look for them! You look for them. You do … at the park, on the bus … where ever … . You know who I'm talking about. You don't wonder … if somebody took the time to roll up *your* turkey? Zip *your* zipper up to the neck? It's just us here. You can admit it to me. I'm not talking about deli meat. I didn't think THAT mother was MY … That *would* be crazy. I'm way too old to be her … I mean, she's obviously not my … but if she was … and if she died, I'd come up with a great memory about her. The way she rolled up the turkey … like she was performing surgery. I wouldn't get sick to my stomach thinking about her. I'd put together a beautiful memorial service. She'd deserve it. That's not why I cried. I cried because … as long as mom was alive … there was always that chance … you know … that hope you hold out even when you know there's no point … that maybe … I'd wake up in the morning and she'd be—this is gonna sound stupid—she'd be … someone else. This stranger in my house would be gone, and my real mother would be there. And my life would finally start. That's how I fell asleep every night in this house … waiting for my real mother. But she's really dead now. She's never gonna turn into someone else at midnight like some fairytale. If I hid it from the world … it's not cuz she wasn't *that* bad … it's cuz it was too awful to admit … even to myself. *(tears up)* I'm not crying. Don't touch me. I'm not giving you a damn hug. I'm not giving you a memory either. Cuz there are none. And stop looking at me like I've got three heads. You're no different than me.

PUDDING
Michael Tooher

Dramatic
Mary, mid-twenties

Mary is aggressively stalking John, a widower twice her age. He deals with his grief by sending single boxes of Jello chocolate pudding to people he picks at random from the telephone book. Mary, who is in marketing, has plans for John. She wants to make him a living logo, The Crazy Pudding Man, for a Jello competitor who is her client. John has just said no and has asked her to leave.

MARY

Go right ahead. Have a heart attack. You should be dead. That's what you want, right? You already have your crypt all laid out here. Look at yourself. Your precious door would make a fine tombstone. *(Pause)* You know, studies have shown that older men who survive their wives don't do so for very long. They sit and grieve and ultimately wither away and die. And quickly too. Which is exactly what you are doing. Tell me, are you happy? Are you content? Is this what you imagined for yourself when you were young? This pathetic existence? You try to fight your loneliness and fear by shutting yourself away here in your pudding tomb. You're so afraid of human contact that you have to reach out through the mail with those sad little boxes. *(Pause)* Then, when God, or Fate or the Great Magnet or whatever you think a higher power is sends me to you, what do you do? You literally shut the door on me. I have to fight my way in. And for what? For who? For you, that's who, for you. And guess what mister? I'm the only person who cares. I'm the person reaching out here. You are ducking and hiding and looking all upset and shocked half the time I'm here. You're afraid of everything. You can't even admit to having the slightest connection to me. Who needs it? *(Pause)* You know what, you are unbelievable. I bring you a rare and amazing opportunity and all you do is cringe and whine. I give you a chance to get out, meet new people, see the world, and yes, make some money. For both you and me. And you deny me. You deny me. Well guess what? I don't have one foot in the grave. I'm young and I'm competent and, yes, I'm hungry. I want things, I want all of it. Houses and cars and clothes and sensations and experience. I want it. And you had the chance to have some of it too. I don't understand you. But you know what? I'm not going to try anymore. You have reached the end of the line with me, mister. Have your heart attack. The only person in your life who gives a shit anymore is leaving. Right now.

For information on this author, click on the WRITERS tab at www.smithandkraus.com.

STET

Kim Davies

Dramatic
Ashley, nineteen

Ashley is a college student being interviewed about her experience as the victim of a sexual assault.

ASHLEY

Okay, um … I … This was last year when I was a freshman, like I think almost in—Almost in just the first month of school, no, I guess the second month … I, um, I thought it was going to be a date … just like a regular date. And I remember all the girls in my dorm were like, how did you get him to ask you out, because guys never ask you on dates, they just want to hook up. And he was a—he was a junior, and I thought he would like … never talk to me. But he was like, do you want to go to this party. *Pause.* So we went to this party at his frat? My first party at college. And, um, I don't really drink—I think I maybe only had like a couple sips of this punch they were giving people, just because … I don't know. I was really dumb. And I think he could tell I was kind of overwhelmed, because he was like, let's go upstairs, it'll be quieter up there, and at the time I wasn't thinking like, oh, he lives upstairs, I wasn't putting that together, I didn't think I was agreeing to go to his room, I just thought he meant it wouldn't be so crowded. And then he was like do you want to see my room, but like really sudden and kind of—pushy?—like we were already walking down the hallway, we were already there before I had a chance to think about it, so I thought, okay, I'll see his room, like I'll step inside, but then I'll say I have to go to the bathroom or something I He didn't turn on the light, like he closes the door and he locks it but he doesn't turn on the light and there are so many guys I There are just so many guys, and I I know something bad is going to happen … *Pause.* They pushed me down, and I hit something—something glass, I think, and it broke, and it cut into me And they kept pushing me down and I tried to get away and someone hit me in the face It was so dark. They um, they held my legs open And, um, you know … Um, they had sex with me.

For information on this author, click on the WRITERS tab at www.smithandkraus.com.

STET

Kim Davies

Dramatic
Christina, twenty-three

Christina is an activist and recent college graduate who now works for her school running its sexual assault victims' services. She is being interviewed about her personal experience with sexual assault.

CHRISTINA

So, um, I went to this party with him, and I got a little drunk. I'd never really gone out drinking before, obviously. And I knew right away, as soon as I started feeling drunk, that I had to go home. And he offered to walk me. And he walked me right into my dorm and up the hallway and right to my door, and my roommate wasn't there. And all of a sudden he started kissing me? And I was really surprised, because I liked him, but he'd very much been playing it cool, you know? Like I had no idea he was interested in me that way, I really just thought he was being nice. I mean, I usually assume—I mean, I think I'm attractive? But like I know I'm not conventionally attractive. So we made out, and that seemed normal … I don't know. It very much—escalated. And I knew I didn't want to have sex, that I didn't want to have sex outside of, like, a relationship. I mean, I didn't have any serious relationships in high school—I guess that's how I knew I didn't want to have sex, because I'd had sex outside of a relationship before and I knew it wasn't for me? It's weird, it's like—I don't really have an emotional relationship with it anymore, so it's not like It's not like hard to talk about It just feels— It's not hard to talk about.

(She takes a breath.)

So he wants to have sex, and I think I said something like, not right now, and he keeps pushing Like literally pushing. And I think I had taken off a lot of my clothes at that point but I had been very much like "my underwear stays on" and um Yeah, it was very weird. It was just very not normal all of a sudden. It was so weird. I was drunk—I mean, I was more drunk than I'd ever been in my life, but I probably wasn't that drunk. But I kept trying to, you know, sort of politely move his hands away from my underwear, and then, you know, less politely

… *(laughs)* I wasn't really—I'm not like a football player, you know? And he actually pushed me down, and I was so dizzy I couldn't—And then, you know, he did it. And I know I said no. He said, later, that I didn't say no, but I know I said no. I know I asked him to stop.

For information on this author, click on the WRITERS tab at www.smithandkraus.com.

THE SADTIC EP
Graham Techler

Comic
Mercer, mid-twenties

Mercer has been asked by two old friends to be the muse that inspires their attempt at an acoustic punk EP. After the sexual tension between the trio reaches a breaking point, Mercer calls a quorum to explain what needs to happen next.

MERCER

Ladies and Gentlemen, I rise today in utter contempt of the empty promises your Punk EP has made this country, of the relentless stagnation of progress, of the utter dearth of insight, arrogant moral bankruptcy, and pointless, juvenile whining that has characterized this project from the word go. As a woman of both pride and prejudice; both sense, and sensibility; of Turner, and also Hooch, I will not sink to *ask* you, but instead simply urge you to make the only rational decision now available to you and warn you of the consequences you invite upon yourself if you reject this option today. Faced as you are with sexual tension, internal jealousy, misplaced affection, interpersonal obsession, extrapersonal obsession, et al, what is of course called to mind is Russell's antinomy, in which he articulated that the "comprehensive class we are considering, which is to embrace everything, must embrace itself as one of its members. In other words, if there is such a thing as "everything," then, "everything" is something, and is a member of the class "everything." But normally a class is not a member of itself. Mankind, for example, is not a man. Form now the assemblage of all classes which are not members of themselves. This is a class: is it a member of itself or not? If it is, it is one of those classes that are not members of themselves, i.e., it is not a member of itself. If it is not, it is not one of those classes that are not members of themselves, i.e. it is a member of itself. Thus of the two hypotheses—that it is, and that it is not, a member of itself—each implies it's contradictory. This is a contradiction." *(Pause)* You need to let me join the band.

SIX BILLION ARCHITECTS

Mark Andrew

Seriocomic
Franny, late thirties

Franny has just told her boyfriend, Lane, that it was a false alarm—she got her period. It's hard being a woman!

FRANNY

All that fuss over a period. My life is like a supermarket dairy product, waiting frantically for my best-before date not to zoom by with a wooosh ... The truth is I won't stop checking my expiration date until I have a little tiny baby boy being looked after by the nanny, waiting for me to come home from designing mother-fucking-boards. I don't know how I'll feel if I have a girl. I'll be equally nanny-fied that's for sure, and equally as blessed, but I'd feel awkward looking her in the eyes. Because she'll have adulthood in front of her. Look in the eyes of a single woman at twenty; she's got so much inner fuel just waiting to be burned: 'Corrupt me! Turn me on to freaky stuff! Meth! Block my windpipe! Just play with me!' But at thirty, those same eyes send a different message: 'Okay, just don't try to burn me, okay?' There's a bit of fuel left in the tank - just enough to get you back for planetary re-entry, should things go horribly pear shaped. But look at those eyes again at forty. There's a distant echo from decades before: 'Use me! Dump me! Turn me inside out! Pick me! Unpick me! Unlock me!' But the fuel's pretty much spent, and you don't want to be exposed to middle-aged men on Viagra, it's exhausting and ... unpoetic, and any guy you meet is going to try and impress you with pinot and sushi in a city bar instead of listen. Sixty seconds after he's dropped you off for the last time, he's singing along to fucking Supertramp on the car radio, putting his ring back on, covering the tan line he doesn't realize you noticed and returning to a suburb with plenty of trees and schools and soccer fields and a wife busy in the tub shaving her legs for him while she mentally flicks through nutritious paella recipes. You're not even a speed bump in his memory lanes.

SIX BILLION ARCHITECTS

Mark Andrew

Seriocomic
Franny, late thirties

Franny expresses her frustration to her boyfriend, Lane, about not having had a baby by her age. He just doesn't get it.

FRANNY

Listening to you is like being run over in slow motion. It's just language to you isn't it? This whole 'interesting' notion of being child-free? Well it's not an academic exercise for me. I don't want to get to the end and be lowered into the ground without these lovely ovaries doing their job. It's what I'm for. I mean, look at me. I'm bloody gorgeous. Isn't that for something? It's supposed to give me an advantage. Except all it's delivered is a guy with a smart mind who's going to intellectualize himself out of the gene pool like a … blind … disabled, drowning swimmer. Could I be a good parent, do I have that intuition; will my child look at me like nature intended? I don't know. I may or may not be a good mother. There's never been anyone to judge. And I'm banging my head on the mommy ceiling. Friends, gloating with menstrual *schadenfreude* when they get knocked up. Chattering on relentlessly with all the, Christ, *nomenclature* of maternity: sonograms, stitches, leaking nipples, how long before you feel like jumping your fella again. I'm outside of it all, like a club I'm barred from. It seems like there's scores of fat stupid cows squeezing out brats like piglets all over town and I'll never know what it feels like.

STONE COLD SOBER

Macee Binns

Dramatic
Maggie, nineteen

Maggie makes one last plea for her father to get help before it's too late.

MAGGIE

I don't know how long you were gone the first time you went to rehab. I know that I was six, and that it didn't work ... obviously. But I do remember the day that you came back. I was playing on the front porch swing when your truck pulled in the driveway, like it was the most natural thing in the world. I closed my eyes and tried to lay there, real still, hoping that you wouldn't see me because I didn't know what I was supposed to do. When you got close to the door I peeked up at you. You looked the same, wearing your stupid muddy water t-shirt and giant white golfing hat. When I saw that I wanted to run up and give you a hug, but I didn't. I didn't, cause I knew that if I did you would tell me that you were sorry and I didn't want to talk about it because I was scared that I would cry, and I didn't want to make you sad. *(Beat)* You know, I think I've been doing that ever since ... trying to avoid talking to you about it because I don't want to hurt you Dad. I mean, your addiction has never been a secret. I've listened to so many people beg you to get sober over the years, and I've always thought that it was just implied that I really wanted you to as well. But the other day I realized, I don't know if I have ever actually said those words to you before. So I'm saying them now. *(Beat)* At Pop's funeral you told me that you were going to try to be a better father for me, and I want you to start right now. Put down the bottle today Dad, please. Do it now, or it will never happen. I'm not naïve, I know that getting sober won't cure you. I can see how sick you are. The damage you've done can't be repaired. I understand that. But it could buy me a little more time with you, and I'll take whatever I can get. It's kind of ironic, you know, Pop fought with everything he had to stay alive for me, and I'm having to beg you to choose to live. I know that you're not afraid to die, but I can't handle the death thing again. Not right now, anyway. *(Beat)* I've never asked you for anything in my whole life, Dad, but I'm begging you now ... please get help. I need you to get better because ... well, for the first time in my life I actually need you right now. I know it's probably not going to happen. I'm not sure if it's even possible for you to get clean after all these years. But I just needed to say it, for me. I need to know that I tried. That I didn't just give up on you. I could never hate you, Dad, even if you fail. But for once in my life I need you to be some kind of normal father. Even if it's only for a little while. I'll take a little while.

For information on this author, click on the WRITERS tab at www.smithandkraus.com.

STUDENT BODY

Frank Winters

Dramatic
Maggie, twenty-one

Maggie, along with several other students, has been called together to deal with a problem: one of them has found a video taken at a party that all of them were at, and towards the end of that video is what might be one of their mutual friends, Cal, sexually assaulting a girl not many of them know beyond her reputation: Laura. Maggie does know Laura, better than anybody else in this room, and only moments ago, Maggie voted not to take it to the cops. When questioned by her older sister, Maggie reveals that not only was she present when this happened, but that she believes it was consensual. In this speech, Maggie tries to convince these upperclassmen - and herself - that nothing happened.

MAGGIE

It wasn't scary and it wasn't violent. It was - beautiful. I mean, they were lying down on, or, well, technically, *she* was lying down on the island in your kitchen, Sarah, like you said, and I just remember thinking, you know, I don't think I've ever seen Laura look so happy before. I mean, he was kissing her, you know. *He* was kissing *her.* *Nobody* kisses Laura Heller like that. Nobody. And I know what you think of her and believe me, she does, too. But she's not, you know, she's not a bad person, she just, she just tries too hard sometimes, because she wants so bad for somebody to like her. To pay attention to her. Like that. And so when I saw her, and he was, you know, he was holding her and kissing her and everything, I mean, I knew it was strange, but after what Sarah had done earlier, I thought, well, maybe it's not, you know? Maybe this is just what happens. And nobody else seemed to find it weird, and they didn't even seem to notice, but, and I know you think she's like this big attention whore and everything but if this video got out and people saw? She would hate that. Seriously. Like, if she even knew that you guys had a tape or that you were talking about her like this? She would hate that. She would lose it. Seriously. So, yeah, if you want my opinion, then, yeah, I think it would be a really bad idea to take this thing to the police. I think Rob was right, you know? I think this might have been the best night of her life. I mean. It was the best night of mine.

For information on this author, click on the WRITERS tab at www.smithandkraus.com.

STUDENT BODY

Frank Winters

Dramatic
Daisy, twenty-two

Daisy is having an awful night. She has watched as nine college students wrestle with a decision: they've found a video of a young man (Cal) sexually assaulting an unconscious young woman (Laura) at a party that they all were at—should they take it to the police or destroy it? To Daisy, the answer is obvious: the young woman was unconscious, therefore she could not give consent, therefore it was rape. You take it to the police. End of story. But for the last hour, she has watched as these people attempted to bully, intimidate, and manipulate one another. She's watched them make specious and repellent arguments about whether or not the young woman could somehow be at fault, judging by the way she behaves and dresses. She's even watched in horror and disgust as people switched sides completely, abandoning their principles, once they'd found out the young man in question is a beloved friend of theirs - among them, her best friend, April. As this monologue begins, Daisy is the last one left who wants to take it to the cops. It's nine against one, and Daisy wants to know this is all going to end.

DAISY

Hey, I'm trying to help you, here. I'm on your side because we both know you aren't gonna let me leave this room until I agree not to say anything, right? Because here's the thing, you are involved now. All of you. You are the story now. And if the cameras and the news trucks arrive, they're not just gonna be looking for Cal or Laura Heller anymore, they're gonna be looking for you. So you need to put a stop to this. Tonight, right, Rob? So, what haven't we tried? Come on, let's really put our heads into this. Do I have a problem of some kind? Could you blackmail me? Do I have a baby in a shoebox somewhere? Or, hey, do you know what I just thought of? There's nine of you. Why don't you just beat the shit out of me. What. Now everybody's all quiet. Have I offended you? Have I offended you, Pete? You wouldn't do something like that, is that it? You're one of the good guys, right? Or actually, and I really don't know why I didn't think of this sooner, Rob, maybe you should call up your old friend Cal and see if he has any suggestions for what to do with a woman when she doesn't want to do what you tell her to do? I'll bet he's got some fucking fantastic suggestions. Why don't we call him, or hey, better yet, why don't you call him, April, and then when he says something you don't wanna hear, you can hang up on him, too. How does that sound?

For information on this author, click on the WRITERS tab at www.smithandkraus.com.

LAWRENCE HARBISON

SUBTENANT

Daniel Hirsch

Dramatic
Computer - female, ageless

Throughout the course of this play, Rick struggles to access the content of his recently deceased son's (Matthew) laptop. Without the correct password Rick can't log on and examine the digital remains of his son's life—a life Rick didn't know well. Through Rick's grief-riddled frustration, the inanimate laptop comes to life and transforms into a sometimes taunting, frequently withholding, though ultimately empathetic presence. In this monologue, the now fully animate, sentient Computer denies Rick access to the digital content of his son's life once again, but offers the grieving father some limited solace.

COMPUTER

I can't do what you're asking, Rick. I can't play you the MP3 files Matthew streamed when he was feeling sad or the playlist he exported to an external device for long bus rides. I can't show you the address book he had regularly synced with his mobile phone—all the names of the contact information of the people he worked with or drank with or played online Scrabble with or loved most. You can't see the location pin he dropped at the all-night diner he visited because he loved to eat their waffles and ice cream when he was a little bit stoned. I can't show you the digital photographs Matthew uploaded after his last visit to the beach, the high res JPEG of an unnamed, smiling figure lying in the sun naked except for a pair of black sunglasses. You can't have access to these things. My sentiment analysis software indicates that you are in deep, deep pain. It must be awful. But this is what it means to be you and not him, to be father and not son. This is what happens when you reach the limits of knowing a user profile, a human person, your boy … But let me say this: the temperature of my motherboard is rising. You can feel my growing heat, you can be illuminated by my glow. You can hold me, Rick. Touch me and you will be touching the smooth surface your son's fingers moved over every day. Condensation from his palms pooled near my mouse pad. Bits of his skin and strands of his hair swept in between my keys. I was with him before he died, his smell is still on me—in me. Touch me and you touch an object your son clutched to his body. Hold me and you hold something the little boy you once held in your arms once held in his.

THE SURROGATE

Patricia Cotter

Dramatic,
Crystal, early twenties

Crystal is a first time surrogate. Due to pregnancy complications, she is forced to fly in from San Diego to San Francisco to spend the last six weeks of her pregnancy with Billy and Sara, the couple who hired her to carry their child. In this monologue an increasingly isolated Crystal shares a dream with Margaret, Billy's best friend. Margaret may or may not have feelings for her.

CRYSTAL

I had a dream last night that an angel came into my room. I was here, sleeping, and I heard this tapping on the window . . . Should I shut up? Is this, like, so so boring? My boyfriend would always tell me his dreams and I hated it. We broke up. He thought it would be a great idea that once I did this baby, that I do another one right away, so that we could pay off his student loans. I was like . . . yeah . . . asking me to pimp out my uterus for your UC San Diego debt? Ummm . . . deal-breaker. So I hear this tapping and I go to the window and this really cute angel, all wavy hair, flowing robes was waving at me to let him inside. And I was just about to open the window when I thought, maybe this was some kind of ploy. Like I'd open the window and he'd turn into something evil. But he seemed sweet, so I just opened it a bit, but when I did he pushed past me and got inside. Once he was in, he wasn't as sweet, he seemed kind of aggressive, like a salesman. He started talking really fast, but it was all gibberish. Did you ever hear anybody speak in tongues? Finally I just said: Can you write it down? And he wrote: "Beggars can't be choosers." What do you think that means?

TAKEN

Susan Jackson

Dramatic
Corrie, forties - sixties

Corrie is speaking to the body of a deceased man in the San Francisco Coroner's morgue. She believes it to be her estranged younger brother, Ben, whom she hasn't seen for eight years. He was kicked out of their home by her husband, Robert, when their daughter Jessie was eight because he was caught using heroin. After losing his job, his boyfriend, and his home, Ben began using again and died of an intentional overdose. Corrie saw the photo of Ben in a newspaper and, against her husband's wishes, journeyed to San Francisco to identify him. It is Ben.

CORRIE

She said I could have some time with you. I guess you heard that. No, of course you didn't. People here are trying to help. And they are … helpful. She said that it's okay that they haven't done the DNA—if I think it's you, it's okay to speak to you. I mean, speak to—. Jessie's going through a rough time. Maybe that's just being sixteen. She seems angry a lot—Robert calls it "teen-age angst." She has this friend Matt who you'd like, I think. He's good in math. I'm happy she's got Matt because she doesn't—Why am I rambling? That's what we do, isn't, Benny? You don't know this, but I looked for you. For six … .no … .three months. And we were robbed. Someone broke in the house and took everything and they destroyed a lot of our things. Tore the place apart. For no apparent reason than just to destroy—But we weren't home and I told Robert, "they're just objects that can be replaced; not like … .people".—we'd been camping and—Why didn't you call me? I'd let you live with us again. I would. We kept your room. I mean, we didn't keep it like someone who … It's a guest room. I still have boxes of your things. Jessie drew pictures of you until she … . didn't. Robert told her you'd gone on a long trip. I wish you had. You should have become a monk. Even if we never saw you again, I'd know you were okay. Taken care of by a bunch of monastic guys cleaning gold and saying prayers waiting to go to heaven. Even if they are a bunch of wooly misogynists, I don't care. At least you'd be safe. At least you'd be … Benny. I miss you. I miss what you were. I miss you … I miss us. *(pause)* Me.

For information on this author, click on the WRITERS tab at www.smithandkraus.com.

THE TALENTED ONES

Yussef El Guindi

Dramatic
Cindy, late twenties

Cindy is speaking to her husband, Omar. Omar, returning home, had witnessed her making out with his good friend Rick.

CINDY

How long were you watching? - You know something, I don't care. I'm not explaining myself to you. It's you who needs to explain when exactly you were going to tell me you'd been fired? When I couldn't pay our bills? - So your buddy came on to me and for a brief second I felt turned on by that. Big fucking deal. Shoot me for wanting to live a little for the first time in months. Did you hear the part where I said no because I love you? I don't know why I bother. I don't know what it is about me that makes people think they can take advantage. You're like my family: The more I give, the more they expect from me. That's my job: provider, cook, translator, and all-purpose doormat. And look what you brought from the grocery: it's all for you: Oreos, beer, soda, chips, beef-jerky, none of this is food. No wonder I almost made out with Rick. Maybe if you spent more time with me I wouldn't be feeling like there's a big gaping hole that needs filling if just to stop me from fucking screaming all the time.

(Unexpectedly, she becomes a little teary.)

And you know something . . . it did feel wonderful - to have someone want me again. I feel like a complete lump all day, and you don't help me feel any different.

THE TALENTED ONES

Yussef El Guindi

Dramatic
Cindy, late twenties

Cindy is arguing with her husband Omar about the pros and cons of having become a U.S. citizen. The "brilliant day" she refers to is the swearing in ceremony when they both became U.S. citizens. Their argument is a "dark night of the soul" moment for both of them, where they have to decide if they want to stay together as a couple.

CINDY

You think I've betrayed something? What have I sold out to? Enlighten me. Have I failed to carry some memory of hurt the way you do with your father? I don't need to remember that kind of pain to function, that's your gig. Forgetting is healthy. That's the beauty of getting to this country. We *can* reinvent everything. Don't blame me if you can't do it as well as I can. I *do* remember that brilliant day. You had the look of someone who had received the best news ever. I wanted to get next to that person because I felt it too. I'm doing great thank you very much. In spite of everything. I'm sorry your family had it particularly bad. Whose family didn't get treated like second class citizens because they'd just got here, because they *had* just got here. We all had to twist ourselves into people we're not to get ahead. That's not a bad thing. It's called adapting. And the price for it is just fine as far as I'm concerned. I like my house. I like the lotions I buy so I can be soft enough to make you want to touch me, you ungrateful prick. And yes, I am a fucking success. I may have to get a second job, and I don't know what the fuck we're going to do about next week's bills, but I *am* succeeding. In spite of still being considered a second class citizen by some people. I had a patient tell the doctor the other day that he didn't want someone like me touching him. You want to know why I haven't pursued my dancing? Because the thought of it, which is so alive in me, the dream of it keeps me going. Maybe I have been afraid to drag it out into the real world, because it's the only pure thing I can hang onto, and I don't want it soaking up the toxic fumes you live off. God forbid my muse should become as fucked up as yours, screaming at the world *all the time*. But you know something: I do want to make room for what I love now. And you know something else, of the two of us, I have been the real artist. I've taken a shit sandwich and turned it into something nurturing. I'm the one taking a lousy story and giving it the happy ending I deserve. Because I've fucking earned it. And if you can't be my partner in that then maybe you should just go. Go away and fucking die yourself.

THE TANGO

Elayne Heilveil

Seriocomic
Sheilah, late thirties-fifties

_Sheilah has come to apply for a tango lesson and is talking to Emmanuel
(Manny), the instructor, to sign up for some classes. She is a bit wry and
self-deprecating, but with charm._

SHEILAH

I thought I should do something I was scared of. I mean I was thinking of sky diving, but thought maybe I should start with the tango. It
is complimentary, right? I could sign for more … but I just have to
warn you, I have commitment issues. I was thinking … you know,
coming home at night. I'm up at six AM, feed the cats, then water the
plants, eat of course, something simple …

(Indicates less than perfect body.)

… clearly not simple enough … And then, the bus to the train and into
a little cubicle all day long where I proof read books, mostly texts, to
find mistakes. That's me. The Shame Buster. Always looking, looking,
for mistakes. No matter how much someone thinks it's perfect, there
is ALWAYS something. An excessive verb, a misplaced noun, non
sequiturs that lead absolutely nowhere. Even if it's just a little comma,
an extra elipsis, an apostrophe gone wrong, a whole world of meaning
can just … fall apart. Right before your eyes … Please don't look at
me. Anyway, by the end of the day, you can imagine, I get back on
the train and just … stare. But every night, when it gets dark, I see the
sign, Manny's Tango, on the second floor. And well, sometimes, I can
see someone up here, dancing. And it's like I'm peeking in … inside,
the window of … I don't know, it's silly, I just see him … dancing.
Alone. And I imagine … I'm sorry. It really _is_ silly. But I imagine that
… it could be me. That they are waiting for … me. That there is this
… window … of 'opportunity'. I said it was silly but I think, Sheilah,
get off the train. Go, now! Dance! Live! Do … _something_. I mean it's
not exactly like I'm alone. Without a partner. I mean there is a Steve. I
come home every night and sit on the couch and stare at TV. And just
the other night, with Steve … Oh no, he's just another Steve. There

was Steve One. Ten years ago. Steve Two. Two years after that. And now, Steve Three. I know it's strange. But always, there is something … wrong … with the Steves. I mean, they're very nice. But it could be just a little thing, like the way a piece of lettuce gets stuck in a tooth. Or the way their hands lay limp in mine. I just find … something. And year after year, I just sit there, on New Year's eve and watch the ball drop and count down another year. Five, four, three, two … to what? Another year of wrong words, wrong Steves, wrong … me's. And I think, is this it? Is this all? Is this what my life is? And then I think of that someone. In the window. I said it was silly. And I don't know what I was thinking. It was just a dream. I know nothing of this world. This dance. This way of being. But … I got off the train. And came here. To find … ? Something. Someone? Dancing?

(Looks at him; is it him?)

Dancing … in the window?

For information on this author, click on the WRITERS tab at www.smithandkraus.com.

THIS RANDOM WORLD

Steven Dietz

Dramatic
Claire, twenty-nine

Claire's boyfriend has told her that he is breaking up with her. This is her response.

CLAIRE

Oh, I see: you get to have final words but I don't? Isn't that why we came here today? It sure wasn't for the food. didn't we come here to listen to your final words to me, Gary?And we are bowing our heads . . . And we are closing our eyes . . . Before the closing of this lid—n this rainy day in February let us mark for one another this moment: Close your eyes, Gary. This lone section of quesadilla—these humble four inches of salt and flour and water and cheese . . . this represents the very last thing that Gary and Claire will ever share in this world. So let us properly mark the moment here today when Gary told Claire it was over. And the next moment when Claire asked Gary why. And the moment after that when Gary said it seemed like Claire could not be "present"—truly present with him because she is filled with what Gary calls "misplaced nostalgias" —because she still talks about high school and childhood and growing up way too much—as though she were stuck in the past—and if Claire is already stuck like that, how will she and Gary ever look to the future! Live the moment! Carpe The Diem and All That?! And let the record note that Claire said: Okay, Gary. Maybe you're right. Give me another chance. Let's give it one more try. And Gary said . . . And you said No. You said: We've tried for more than a year. It didn't work. I don't think we should try anymore. And I said: Man, it's really raining out there. We're going to get soaked. And you didn't say anything. And I said: Thehell with it—I don't care if I get soaked. I need to go. And I stood up. And here, Gary —here is where I was waiting for you to say something really Great. I was thinking to myself "God he could say something really Great right here —and maybe that would change everything—maybe we'd still work things out." I know that's unfair. I know there was no way for you to know it was time to come up with the Awesome Thing and Say It—but right there, Gary. . .that was the time for you to say

Something Great. And you said . . . You should box that up. There are homeless people around the corner. You should give that food to them." *(Pause)* I suck at life, Gary. I suck big time. Here I am thinking about my little shattered heart when there are people with nothing to eat. Thank

you for reminding me of that. And thank you for bringing me to a shitty restaurant for our break-up. I should have seen it coming. We've walked by this place so many times and we always said: God, what a pit. We always joked that people should break up at shitty places they were never gonna want to visit again. Because of the memories . . . The way that goodbyes . . . The way that endings just . . . stick to a place . . . Will you please go now? Pleasego—and give the homeless people this food —and leave me alone so I can have a good cry, you asshole.

TOLSTOY IN NEW JERSEY

Sam Bobrick

Comic
Glenda, late twenties to mid-thirties

Glenda Smith, a very confused young woman. finds herself now caught between two lovers. She addresses the audience as to what her needs once were and now are.

GLENDA

Why is it that everything I touch turns to crap? I learn how to drive, I run over my baby brother. At the high school prom my date falls off the hotel roof. And it's not just little things. It's everything in general. Sometimes I think I was put on earth just to give God a good laugh.

(looking up to God)

Well, the joke is over and I don't get it.

(to audience)

It's really not that much I want out of life.

(Produces a paper.)

Here's a list I made out not too long ago, before I was really aware of my true needs.

(Reads.)

Number one on the list, a man.

(to audience)

I'm not so sure about that any more. They seem to be a very confused breed. Always having to try to prove themselves. Stop it and grow up. Either a man is a man or he isn't. If he is, he is. If he isn't, he isn't. So what's the big mystery? Number two on my list . . .

(Looks at list.)

Kids? I must have been drunk when I made this list. To be very honest, kids today, no, I don't think so. If you don't know enough about who you are, why would you even give a shit about who they are? So number two is in the trash can.

(Looks at list.)

Number three, a career.

(to audience)

Doing what? I hate computers and I despise people. Where do I go with skills like that? The DMV? Great, I'll stand on my feet all day long and get varicose veins. No thank you. Number four . . .

(Looks at list.)

A BMW convertible. So far that's the only thing that still makes sense. The bottom line is that some people are luckier than other people. It's that simple.

TRANSit

Darren Canady

Dramatic
Veronica, Late twenties-early thirties, transgender

VERONICA

No, baby, one thing you are NOT is new. Trust Lalo, you're like everything I've EVER done. I know about the South Bronx. Brown boys with city sweat drippin off em. Boys with black-brown eyes that maybe draw you in maybe trap you. Boys with high behinds they can't hide with saggin pants. Talkin street and yellin bullshit. Boys makin the street an obstacle course. Boys that stumble in to sayin that one thing at maybe that one time you're in so much need to hear somethin' good and fresh and sweet and maybe a little nasty that they catch your ear. Boys who keep throwin out lines til they find that somethin that works. I see 'em all in you. How you tryin your swagger out on me. You keep diggin in your mind's tool box, your mental bag of tricks to see what's gonna tease me open. Get me to let you in. Let you ride with me. Get more minutes get more dances get some glances. Lookin for some cheap chat that's the front door to my place. I ain't said a goddamn thing 'bout what I got or what I ain't got. I told you I know boys. Y'all the ones think you're irresistible. See I know boys and their feelings, too. Sensitive boys. City boys. Stopped and frisked boys. Brown boys who don't think nobody see 'em. But I see you. See you tryin' to turn a buck - make some jumps and flips on the subway buy you some food or some rent or some clothes. See you and cry for you a little. Feel sorry for you from a distance. Watch you get beat down til having functioning hearts and minds is a danger. And under the slick sly swagger there's rage and confusion and muscle and sinew and love and sex. Sensitive, sensitive boys. Are you one of those boys, Lalo? Does that sound like you?

VAUDEVILLE

Laurence Carr

Seriocomic
Yvette, thirties to forties

Yvette, a second tier vaudeville performer, plays out her dream career in
the parlor of a Philadelphia theatrical boarding house in 1919.

YVETTE

They settled the actors' strike. I'm giving my notice. I'm off the circuit.
I'm leaving tonight after the show. I've got to get back to New York.
The legit show'll be casting Monday morning. What's everybody
looking at? You'd all leave Vaudeville in second if George White of
Flo Ziegfeld wired you. Who wouldn't want to be in The Scandals
or The Follies. Or in a play where you're out there being a person. It
beats split weeks and two-a-day. I want a normal life. I want to get up
at noon, bathe 'til two, have my lunch brought up on a cart. Nap 'til
six. Have my maid wake me and dress me. Have my chauffeur drive
me down to 42nd Street, go up to my dressing room, my dressing
room, the one with the star. I want to water my roses. I want to put
on make-up that doesn't make me smell like a stockyard. I want my
stage manager to knock softly on my door and say, "Half-hour will be
whenever you say it is, Miss Ogg." Finally, I'll prepare for my entrance.
I'll stand in the wings, feeling for that moment they've waited so long
for. Saved their pennies for. And when this happens, I'll walk through
that door. A real door, like this. Not a painted canvas with a split in
it. I'll walk onto the set that looks like a room, a real room. With real
pictures on the wall, and a real table with a real lace tablecloth, and a
lamp I can turn on and off, and a chair that's a chair, and a real carpet
on the floor. Then, I'll play a scene that'll make everybody cry. And
everybody'll say, "That poor girl. If only some of life's beauty could
have been given to her." And I would die on that stage. Alone. And
they'd forget all about Little Eva. Then, the curtain would fall—no—it
would descend. And there'd be silence. And then, from the back of the
house, my manager would start the applause. And it would grow. And
the audience would realize that what they just saw wasn't real—it just
felt so real. They'd remember that this was a play, and the star had
just emptied herself on that stage, and now it was up to them to bring

her back to life. And I'd take eight or ten curtain calls, begging them to let me go. Then, back to my dressing room to receive friends and favors and the gentlemen of the press, to whom, "I shall always be grateful for your many kind words." Then to Delmonico's for a late supper of quail and champagne, petit pois and roasted potatoes. Then off to a club to catch Sophie Tucker's last few songs. She bows to me. And then home to bed, because in the morning, the great English impresario comes to call to plan my European tour. *(Pause)* I'm not asking for the moon! I just want a normal life.

For information on this author, click on the WRITERS tab at www.smithandkraus.com.

WASTE LAND
Don Nigro

Seriocomic
Vivienne, thirty-two

Vivienne Eliot, wife of the soon to be famous poet T. S. Eliot, has been left behind in Paris in the company of Eliot's friend Ezra Pound, who has promised to look after her while Eliot goes to Switzerland to consult a specialist about his troubled mental state and try to finish the poem that will become The Waste Land. Their marriage has not been going well, and that's part of the reason Eliot is so troubled. Vivienne has been having her own mental problems, and is both frustrated by her unsatisfying relations with her enigmatic and secretive husband and terrified that she is going to lose him. Here Pound has brought her to dinner with the great Irish writer James Joyce, the American writer Gertrude Stein, and Miss Stein's companion, Alice B. Toklas. Vivienne is very smart, very funny, nervous, uneasy, and in increasing distress. As the others look on uneasily, she talks compulsively to take her attention from her growing fear that she is losing her husband forever.

VIVIENNE

Actually, Tom is in Lausanne, having a nervous breakdown. Or recovering from a nervous breakdown. It's always one or the other. Usually both. I just bundled him off on the train. There is something so emotionally complex about French train stations. I stood there feeling as if somebody had just whacked me over the head with a shovel. You're smiling and waving and smiling and waving and trying to be supportive when you feel like a balloon animal with a slow leak, and the air is hissing out your ears until the train's got smaller and smaller and so have you, and you know in your heart the person you love is secretly relieved to have got rid of you. And now here I am in Paris in the rain, and Ezra has been very kind, and it's so good to meet you, Mr Joyce, and Miss Stein and Miss Toklas. Paris is lovely, even soaking wet, but, I can't help asking myself what exactly I'm doing here. Waiting. Waiting for what? I don't know. And why are the French always looking at you as if you just farted? Or as if they farted, but somehow it's your fault? But I don't blame them. I feel like they know how to live and we don't. And I ask myself, how did I get to this place? I can't remember if I've washed my hands or not. I probably have. I wash my hands compulsively. Tom and I are both obsessively clean. He considers it normal on his part and neurotic on mine. Sometimes he wears green makeup. It looks like an avocado exploded in his face. I love my husband very much and hope someday to actually meet him.

WASTE LAND

Don Nigro

Dramatic
Vivienne, thirty-nine

Time: early 1930's
T. S. Eliot's first wife, Vivienne, is gradually becoming more and more emotionally distraught over the rapidly deteriorating state of her marriage. Eliot is now a famous poet editing his own magazine and friends to the London literary elite, but Vivienne feels left out and talked about behind her back. Virginia Woolf has referred to her privately as a bag of ferrets around Tom's neck. Vivienne even suspects that their good friend Ezra Pound turned against her. Her husband's coldness and her growing frustration seem to be slowly driving her mad.

VIVIENNE

Hell is a city much like London. The brown fog creeping down the street. Blurred gas lamps. Monstrous shadows. Time is very strange here, in this place. In this particular circle of Hell. The light of the kiln fires of Hell makes lurid smears on the fog. Who am I quoting now? Hell seems to be full of mad people. Love is a bundle of mirrors. We employ the method of luminous detail, applied apparently at random, but actually not. And Tom is quite famous now. He has his own magazine, which he has very graciously allowed me to help him edit. My job is to write the filler between the masterpieces, a task I perform under a number of assumed and slightly ridiculous names. Like Tom, I am now many different imaginary people. He has spent his life constructing a hall of mirrors to get lost in. A small room may be made to seem much larger by the careful placement of mirrors in odd corners. I have moved from isolation to entanglement to isolation. I can hear the wind going in the mulberry trees. God whispering to himself in his madness. I overheard Ezra telling someone Tom would probably be happier if somebody would either run off with or murder his wife. Unless I dreamed it. I do have strange dreams in this place. But either way, he was joking, of course. I think he was joking. With Ezra, sometimes it's difficult to tell. Ezra's been saying crazier and crazier things. His eccentricity is slowly veering into something else. He makes his own furniture, which comes out as crooked as his poems, hurts your back and gives you splinters in your ass, and plays tennis like a man trying to murder a flying monkey. And yet I'm the one Tom thinks is not quite right. It's true I'm afraid of taxis. Because terrible things happen in taxis. People are trapped and never get out. In my dream, Tom puts on green makeup and takes a taxi to the theatre. He's the Green Man. Then when he gets home we cut him into tiny little pieces which I bury in the rose garden to see if they'll sprout. It's like sleeping with a dug up corpse. Christ was mistaken for a gardener. What he planted was himself. And three days later, he came up. You must not be misled by my husband's newfound piety. Poetry is a kind of demonic possession. Any attempt to make it rational is pure misdirection. The moths gather at the back window by the woods at night. They've come to eat me. They are the souls of all those I have loved. All dead now. All dead. They will find me drowned in a birdbath full of tears. Fear death by water.

WASTE LAND

Don Nigro

Seriocomic
Miss Stein, fifties

MISS STEIN

Well, at least the storm's let up a bit. But I'm not afraid of being struck by lightning. It's all a matter of will power. Oh, my dear. Such a fuss. Such madness and confusion. It is very much like opera with only a bit less screaming. One might think you know that marital advice from a person such as myself might not be entirely welcome considering I am not exactly married, at least not that I care to recall, and do not generally recommend having intimate relations with the male of the species if it can possibly be avoided and yet you know I do have relations and it is I think much the same thing except for the fact that men are not entirely human which we can observe in my friend Hemingway for example who is sometimes a nice and rather talented boy but also a very angry and aggressive and jealous and insecure individual who is excited by the ritual murder of bulls which I do not entirely comprehend although your husband is not very much like Ernest except in that he also is intelligent and has a penis I suppose although I myself have not seen it but let us presume this to be the case and of course Alice B. Toklas does not have a penis at least not usually and yet I have had occasional difficulties which might surprise you because love you see is the same everywhere although always different and is not something which makes sense, which has a grammar which can be properly declined or conjugated because it is something the mystery of which by its very geography defies reason and I have observed my friend Picasso for example treating women like the chewing gum on the bottom of his sandal but this is not love and Picasso although a genius perhaps of some sort or other does not know how to love because a genius can also be a charlatan and a fool because you know so often to love is to embrace a series of humiliations which is impossible to avoid I think people being essentially talking monkeys and men being worse. But you know, no matter what happens, no matter how ridiculous or humiliating or painful, in the end one is always fortunate to have loved. One is lucky to have had the experience of love. Of that there is absolutely no question. To be loved back, however, is a mixed thing. Like mixed nuts.

WARSONG

Gregory Strasser

Dramatic
Ming Jackson, sixty-one, Chinese American

Ming has been convicted of murdering Marcy Gray. Her son Harry has been trying to exonerate her. He has told her that he thinks his sister Olivia was the murderer. Ming denies this; but in doing so, makes it clear that Harry is right.

MING

Think about what you're going to do. From the beginning, Olivia was … was delicate. She was beautiful. My greatest dream. All come true. Everything about her, it was true. And I didn't—you know I didn't know. The dance lessons, the scholarships, the contests … I didn't expect all that. I never imagined that she would become … so amazing. And I told myself I was on the right path: something my mother had failed at. I would not fail my daughter like my mother failed me. I lost sight of things. And so yes, I pushed her. But … one thing that is true: I ruined Olivia's life. I killed it. I took dance from her and killed it. I drove her to try to commit suicide. The night the hospital called us, I didn't sleep for days. I had … become the very thing I sought to avoid. You know your father told me that Olivia hated me? That she was afraid of me? My own daughter … thought of me as a monster. *(Beat)* Olivia did not kill Marcy. And I'll tell you why. Because I killed them both. I killed Olivia and I killed Marcy. The day Olivia died, on the drive home from Toronto, was the day I knew that I was her murderer. The night Marcy was killed, I was there. In every moment. I was in your sister's eyes every second of that night. She could see me. And when I came home and I saw her, I knew it. Marcy was dead. But Olivia was alive again. I could hear her heart: it was beating again. And so when I found my hairbrush out of place, or realized I had forgotten my cell phone, I did not question it. Not for a moment. Because a sacrifice was made that night and it resurrected my daughter. So who killed Marcy Gray? I did. It was me. I did it.

WEAPON OF MASS IMPACT, Part II

Brett Neveu

Dramatic
Kate, thirties

Kates is speaking to a Man and Another Man, two corporate trainers in terrorism avoidance dressed up and play-acting as if they were Kate's captors. She is attempting to remember a memorized speech that covers what one's supposed to say when one's been kidnapped by a terrorist.

KATE

I'm Kate Nichols and I work for Las Cruces Machine. I've been kidnapped and the men who kidnapped me would like my company to pay them $500,000 to let me go. One of the men also tells me that an American killed his brother, Manuel Belizon. An American shot Manuel Belizon in the back, and that they would also like to kill me in revenge for this murder. It outrages me that my country would send a man to another country to murder an innocent. America's power oversteps its bounds and its "policing" strategy is nothing more than an excuse to conduct terrible crimes. These men I am here with seem upstanding and promise to release me upon payment. They tell me they will kill me if they do not receive the money or may kill any of a number of other Americans they have held here. So please do what you can to get the money together to secure my release and also as payment for their dead brother. *(beat)* I'm doing okay, they are treating me fine. Please do not worry. Do as they say. I'm sure there will be contact information along with this so that you will know what to do next. Tell my family and friends I love them. Goodbye.

WEAPON OF MASS IMPACT, Part II

Brett Neveu

Dramatic
Kate, thirties

Kate is speaking to Sylvia, a fellow attendee of a corporate-sponsored retreat on avoiding/confronting global terrorism. She is making somewhat small talk with Sylvia as they work together to complete an exercise about being followed by a dangerous stranger.

KATE

These are good methods they're showing us, I think, so far at least. You know what you should always do, though? When you take a trip? Here's something else you should do: Always tell yourself that when you're away from home, even at a conference or training or something, like for me, if I'm someplace like Cosamaloapan Del Carpio or somewhere, I always tell myself that I'm me and I'll come out of whatever it is without any type of scar. I make an effort to make myself singularly present so that I will not and cannot be shaken. When you are in Germany, France and England, you should do that, you should tell yourself everything is within your grasp. That you are Sylvia from Grayslake and nobody can do anything to you because you're made of super-strong stuff. You should tell yourself you're made of super-strong stuff. I'm not joking. If you personally come across like some sort of confused and insecure idiot with no thought about how you might be getting from point A to point B then you'll find yourself scooped up and dumped into some flaming pile of international crap or worse, you could get severely hurt or maimed and end up in some hospital somewhere where services are questionable and the people unskilled. You should also understand that you should enter whatever new and different situation with all the facts always at hand. If you go somewhere with nothing in your brain, you'll end up with something, and something you don't want. What you have to do is go in with something to begin with, which would be your own personal self-reliance. If you go in with your own ideas of who to trust and who to avoid, what you want to do and what you can leave to the locals and how to get to where you need to go and back again without depending on those you can't even try to understand, you'll come out of the whole thing with something fresh and wonderful—something you wanted, something very, very satisfying. Doesn't that sound good?

WEAPON OF MASS IMPACT, Part II

Brett Neveu

Dramatic
Gina, forties

Gina is speaking to Sylvia, a fellow attendee of a corporate-sponsored retreat on avoiding/confronting global terrorism. While working together to complete an exercise at the retreat, Gina relays a graphic story of loss to Sylvia, a woman she has just met and who has confided in Gina about her own father's death.

GINA

My mom went a month right after my dad. But not because she was sad or alone or anything or she got sick. She had Alzheimer's, actually, but she was functioning fine. She was hearty, she walked by herself around, she'd eat her food on her own. Sometimes she'd even get in a word or two that made some sense. She died though after a care-giver in her facility sexually assaulted her then beat her skull in. She died afterwards in the hospital from loss of blood and severe head trauma. This care-giver guy that did it worked at her facility and I guess the guy was just waiting for my dad to die so he could then slip in there and have sex with my mom. He was a real piece of work. The guy actually came to my father's funeral. He told me that he and my father had been close. He hugged us all afterwards, my mom my sisters and me. Jesus, the jackass was in tears. Later, after he raped and killed my mother—thank god she was demented and didn't know what the hell was going on—he said that he had beat her because she had started to make sounds, sort of yelling when he was doing it, I guess, so he wanted her to be quiet so he covered her mouth but I guess she was still being loud so he tried to knock her out a bunch of times with a coffee mug. He said that over the course of the night that he had sex with her three times. The next morning another care-giver found the guy in the bed asleep next to her, all curled up by her side, asleep.

WHAT WE'LL DO

Sheila Callaghan

Dramatic
Young Woman, twenties

A young woman fantasizes about a man.

YOUNG WOMAN

We'll send aloof, coded emails to each other all day. Beneath the words we type will lie a bed of burning coals, but neither of us will mention it. We'll agree to call one another that night. We do. I don't like talking to you on the phone, you are quiet and I always load the silences with rusted nails. But we do, and it's done. We'll meet on our bikes outside your apartment at 8, your shitty apartment next to the junkie, we'll meet there tonight outside your door, behind the 7-11, we'll meet there. We do. Head out on out bikes, the sun bleeding low behind the Hollywood hills, we ride along Sunset Boulevard, you ahead of me, I'm staring at the checked shirt you bought when we went shopping at a thrift store on Melrose long before we ever touched, I'm staring at your back and your heels in sandals and your hair blowing back, and a song by The Wedding Present is playing in my head as I pedal, and somehow I know this ride is not happening, that you are not happening … We turn into the strip mall and lock our bikes to a post, enter the red dark bar and order Wild Turkeys without ice, and I understand this is the moment I will learn how to be a drunk, I am doing it for you like I learned to drink my coffee black, like I dyed my hair black, like I changed the way I walk, everything is drenched in you and I can't bend from it and I don't care, and if the not-caring is the worst of it then I know I will be fine … but it isn't … Sitting across from you in the bar at a small round table, I will smoke all your cigarettes and twist beneath your silences and I will make my eyes screech with mischief hoping you'll ask me what all the noise is about, and I will suddenly have the sensation we are still pedaling with the sunset behind us, but now the road tips down and our feet fly from the pedals and the pedals spin furiously, and the sky goes black and the cars disappear and all I feel is the terror of not stopping and LA is hot against my skin and you with your checked shirt flapping open before me, and nothing will stop this terror … Then we will finish drinking. Then we will finish smoking. We will leave the bar. Back on our bikes riding toward your shitty apartment, our wheels will wobble because we are drunk and now I ride in front and I stand on my pedals and the wind in my face tells me all I need to know about this night … it tells me the sex will be bad because we've been drinking too much … it tells me I will wake up on your carpet next to you, long before you do, and I will stare at you until I've lost my fucking name … it tells me we will not have breakfast together on your balcony that morning, nor the morning after … and if I had any sense I would ask that wind to tell me the story of the rest of you. But I do not.

WHAT WE'RE UP AGAINST

Theresa Rebeck

Dramatic
Eliza, late twenties - thirties

Eliza is supposed to be on a team of architects designing a new mall, but she has been left out of the loop because the men on the team don't like her, She has managed to get ahold of the plans and solved a tricky problem the team has been working on for months, then put the team leader's name on it. She is having dinner with David, the boss, who hired her and who is unaware of the dynamic of the shenanigans going on. What should she tell him?

LIZA

Okay. Look. Like I said, I'm sorry, you guys. But I do, I have to know where I stand here. I've been here five months and I, it's just, because this isn't going to fly anymore. And I'm having dinner with David tonight, he's been such a supporter of mine and I am going, right now, to meet him for dinner and he is going to want to know what I'm working on and I don't want to say, to him, you know, I'm not working on anything because Stu hates me and I've been shut out of even the lamest projects he has. I don't want to tell him that. But what the fuck, why should I protect you guys? I just came in here and humiliated myself and you're like just, you're not giving me a shitload of motivation to protect you. Why would I? Why would I cover up this bullshit? David's not in Chicago. He got hung up in some meeting with the clients on that restaurant thing over by the stadium, so he ended up pushing his flight till tomorrow. And he and I missed each other this morning because of course you guys were all mad at me so no one told me he was here, so when he got stuck here for an extra night he called me, and he's heading back here because he wants to have a meeting with me so he can hear about how it's going and we can catch up. So what the do you want me to tell him, Stu? What the fuck do I say?

For information on this author, click on the WRITERS tab at
www.smithandkraus.com.

WORLD BUILDERS

Johnna Adams

Seriocomic
Whitney, thirties

Whitney is participating in a clinical drug trial for a medication treating the symptoms of schizoid personality disorder. Here, she tells Max, another patient, about her vivid fantasy world.

WHITNEY

My world is a futuristic dystopia. The Earth has been destroyed by a giant meteorite, thrown at the planet by an alien race that is our enemy. There are seven colony worlds that Earth's survivors fled to. Having cross-bred with native species on several worlds, humanity now has a variety of forms and we live peaceably with several alien races. So, racial subsets have now created seventy-two alien-human hybrid races. There are forty-seven major characters and one hundred and thirty minor characters. This is so hard. How do you describe a world? It isn't a story with a beginning, middle and end. It's a world. I'll start with the earliest world stories from when I was in junior high, and the world first coalesced into a coordinated whole. The torture and execution of Marvina of Taurus Seven! Marvina was a space pirate and a princess and a water-breathing amphibious archeologist. Okay, that's a little unrealistic, sure. But I was twelve when I first made her up. She went on a quest to find the ruins of an underwater alien city to retrieve an artifact that would save humanity from being enslaved by robots this one time. And she met and fell in love with the high priest of a dark cult of demon-worshipping opera singers. And they had three sons. Mikor, Sebastian and Dorrick. Marvina found the artifact and saved humanity and settled down to raise the boys as a single mother. Only this other cult-a demon-worshipping rival cult of belly dancers-wanted to kill her sons. So she killed the belly dancing cult leader and got arrested by the planetary governing council headed by Vernonian the Cursegiver. And it shouldn't have been a big deal because it was in self-defense. But Vernonian used the arrest as an excuse to put Marvina into a trial of mortal combat with a special executioner-android trained to torture and kill amphibious races in a water arena- Glibtrar Drathmek! And so Marvina got thrown into this water arena to fight

Glibtrar to the death. And it was televised and her sons watched as she was tortured and murdered. And there was nothing they could do. So, from there, my fantasy world branched off into three different stories of personal vengeance. Because Mikor, Sebastian and Dorrick were sent in disguise to three different colony worlds out of fear that Vernonian, having killed their mother would come after them next. Do you want to hear about Mikor, Sebastian or Dorrick next?

RIGHTS & PERMISSIONS

ALIVE AND WELL © 2016 by Kenny Finkle. Reprinted by permission of Beth Blickers, Agency for the Performing Arts). For performance rights, contact Broadway Play Publishing, 212-772-8334, www.broadwayplaypubl.com

THE ARSONISTS © 2016 by Jacqueline Goldfinger. Reprinted by permission of Amy Wagner, Abrams Artists. For performance rights, contact Amy Wagner (amy.wagner@abramsartny.com)

BED © 2015 by Sheila Callaghan. Reprinted by permission of Chris Till, Creative Artists Agency. For performance rights, contact Chris Till (ctill@caa.com)

THE BELLE OF BELMAR © 2016 by Nicole Pandolfo. Reprinted by permission of Nicole Pandolfo. For performance rights, contact Nicole Pandolfo (nicole.e.pandolfo@gmail.com)

BIG CITY © 2016 by Barbara Blumenthal-Ehrlich. Reprinted by permission of Barbara Blumenthal-Ehrlich. For performance rights, contact Barbara Blumenthal-Ehrlich (barbaretc@aol.com)

BIG SKY © 2016 by Alexandra Gersten-Vassilaros. Reprinted by permission of ICM Partners. For performance rights, contact Ross Weiner (rweiner@icmpartners.com)

BIRDS OF A FEATHER © 2016 by June Guralnick. Reprinted by permission of June Guralnick. For performance rights, contact June Guralnick (june@juneguralnick.com)

THE BLAMELESS © 2016 by Nick Gandiello. Reprinted by permission of Alexis Williams. Bret Adams Ltd. For performance rights, contact Alexis Williams (awilliams@bretadamsltd.net)

BLUE LILA RISING © 2016 by Sheila Callaghan. Reprinted by permission of Chris Till, Creative Artists Agency. For performance rights, contact Chris Till (ctill@caa.com)

BREATHING TIME © 2009 by Beau Willimon, Reprinted by permission of Chris Till. For performance rights, contact Dramatists Play Service, 440 Park Ave. S., New York, NY 10016. 212-683-8960, www.dramatists.com

BYHALIA, MISSISSIPPI © 2016 by Evan Linder, Reprinted by permission of ICM Partners. For performance rights, contact Di Glazer/Ross Weiner, ICM Partners (dglazer@icmpartners.com/ rweiner@icmpartners.com

CAUGHT © 2016 by Christopher Chen. Reprinted by permission of Antje Oegel., AO International Agency. For performance rights, contact Antje Oegel (aoegel@aoiagency.com)

CHARM © 2015 by Philip Dawkins, Reprinted by permission of Beth Blickers, Agency for the Performing Arts. For performance rights, contact Beth Blickers (bblickers@apa-agency.com)

CLOSED WINDOWS, OPEN DOORS © 2016 by Glenn Alterman. Reprinted by permission of Glenn Alterman. For performance rights, contact Glenn Alterman (glennman10@gmail.com)

CONFEDERATES © 2015 by Suzanne Bradbeer. Reprinted by permission of Amy Wagner, Abrams Artists. For performance rights, contact Amy Wagner (amy.wagner@abramsartny.com)

THE COWARD © 2016 by Kati Schwartz. Reprinted by permission of Kati Schwartz. For performance rights, contact Kati Schwartz (schwartz.kati@gmail.com)

DARN IT! DARLA! © 2015 by Lavinia Roberts. Reprinted by permission of Lavinia Roberts. For performance rights, contact Lavinia Roberts (laviniaroberts@yahoo.com)

DAUGHTERS OF THE SEXUAL REVOLUTION © 2016 by Dana Leslie Goldstein. Reprinted by permission of Dana Leslie Goldstein. For performance rights, contact Dana Leslie Goldstein (dana@theatergarden.org)

DINNER AT HOME BETWEEN DEATHS © 2016 by Andrea Lepcio. Reprinted by permission of the author. For performance rights, contact Elaine Devlin (edevlinlit@aol.com)

DRAW THE CIRCLE© 2016 by Mashuq Mushtaq Deen. Reprinted by permission of Susan Gurman, Susan Gurman Agency LLC. For performance rights, contact Susan Gurman (susan@gurmanagency.com)

ELLERY © 2016 by Jennifer O'Grady. Reprinted by permission of Jennifer O'Grady. For performance rights, contact Jennifer O'Grady (jogrady8@optonline.net)

THE ETRUSCAN LOVERS © 2016 by C.S. Hanson. Reprinted by permission of C.S. Hanson. For performance rights, contact C.S. Hanson (cshansonplays@yahoo.com)

FABULOUS MONSTERS © 2016 by Diana Burbano. Reprinted by permission of Diana Burbano. For performance rights, contact Diana Burbano (dianaburbano@icloud.com)

A FUNNY THING HAPPENED ON THE WAY TO THE GYNE-COLOGIC ONCOLOGY UNIT AT MEMORIAL SLOAN-KETTERING CANCER CENTER OF NEW YORK CITY © 2016 by Halley Feiffer. Reprinted by permission of ICM Partners. For performance rights, contact Dramatists Play Service, 440 Park Ave. S., New York, NY 10016 (www.dramatists.com) (212-683-8960)

GABRIEL © 2016 by C. Denby Swanson. Reprinted by permission of C. Denby Swanson. For performance rights, contact C. Denby Swanson (cdenbyswanson@gmail.com)

GORGONS © 2009 by Don Nigro. Reprinted by permission of Samuel French, Inc. For performance rights, contact Samuel French, Inc., 212-206-8990, www.samuelfrench.com.

GREEN-WOOD © 2016 by Adam Kraar. Reprinted by permission of the author. For performance rights, contact Elaine Devlin (edevlinlit@aol.com)

HOORAY FOR HOLLYWOOD! © 2013 by Lisa Soland. Reprinted by permission of Lisa Soland. For performance rights, contact Lisa Soland (lisasoland@aol.com)

HOUSE RULES © 2014 by A. Rey Pamatmat. Reprinted by permission of Beth Blickers, Agency for the Performing Arts. For performance rights, contact Beth Blickers (bblickers@apa-agency.com)

THE JAG © 2016 by Gino DiIorio. Reprinted by permission of the author. For performance rights, contact Elaine Devlin (edevlinlit@aol.com)

KILLING WOMEN © 2014 by Marisa Wegrzyn, Reprinted by permission of Chris Till, Creative Artists Agency. For performance rights, contact Broadway Play Publishing, 212-772-8334, www.broadwayplaypubl.com.

LAB RATS © 2015 by Patrick Gabridge. Reprinted by permission of Patrick Gabridge. For performance rights, contact Patrick Gabridge (pat@gabridge.com)

LAS CRUCES © 2016 by Vincent Delaney. Reprinted by permission of Mark Orsini, Bret Adams Ltd. For performance rights, contact Mark Orsini (morsini@bretadamsltd.net)

LIFE SUCKS © 2016 by Aaron Posner. Reprinted by permission of Beth Blickers, Agency for the Performing Arts. For performance rights, contact Dramatists Play Service, 440 Park Ave. S., New York, NY 10016. 212-683-8960, www.dramatists.com

THE LOVEBIRDS © 2016 by Barbara Blumenthal-Ehrlich. Reprinted by permission of Barbara Blumenthal-Ehrlich. For performance rights, contact Barbara Blumenthal-Ehrlich (barbarablumenthalehrlich@gmail.com)

LOUISE SPEAKS HER MIND © 2016 by Martha Patterson. Reprinted by permission of Martha Patterson. For performance rights, contact Martha Patterson (mpatterson125933@aol.com)

THE LOVEBIRDS © 2016 by Barbara Blumenthal-Ehrlich. Reprinted by permission of Barbara Blumenthal-Ehrlich. For performance rights, contact Barbara Blumenthal-Ehrlich (barbaretc@aol.com)

LULLABYE © 2016 by Michael Elyanow, Reprinted by permission of Beth Blickers, Agency for the Performing Arts. For performance rights, contact Beth Blickers (bblickers@apa-agency.com)

MARIE AND ROSETTA © 2016 by George Brant. Reprinted by permission of Kate Navin, The Gersh Agency. For performance rights, contact Samuel French, Inc., 212-206-8990, www.samuelfrench.com

MIMESOPHOBIA © 2014 by Carlos Murillo. Reprinted by permission of Antje Oegel, AO International Agency. For performance rights, contact Antje Oegel (aoegel@aoiagency.com)

MORNING AFTER GRACE © 2016 by Carey Crim. Reprinted by permission of Carey Crim. For performance rights, contact Carey Crim (careycrim@aol.com)

THE MOVING OF LILLA BARTON © 1989 by John MacNicholas. Reprinted by permission of Earl Graham. For performance rights, contact Earl Graham (grahamacynyc@aol.com)

MY LIFE AS YOU © 2016 by Laura Rohrman. Reprinted by permission of Laura Rohrman. For performance rights, contact Laura Rohrman (nonirohr@gmail.com)

ONEGIN AND TATYANA IN ODESSA© 2016 by Don Nigro. Reprinted by permission of Don Nigro. For performance rights, contact Samuel French, Inc., 212-206-8990, www.samuelfrench.com

OTHER THAN HONORABLE© 2015 by Jamie Pachino. Reprinted by permission of Beth Blickers, Agency for the Performing Arts. For performance rights, contact Beth Blickers (bblickers@apa-agency.com)

PERILOUS NIGHT © 2007 by Lee Blessing. Reprinted by permission of Lee Blessing. For performance rights, contact Lee Blessing (leeblessing@gmail.com)

PLANCHETTE © 2016 by Carolyn Gage. Reprinted by permission of Carolyn Gage. For performance rights, contact Carolyn Gage (carolyn@carolyngage.com)

PLUCKER © 2016 by Alena Smith, Reprinted by permission of ICM Partners. For performance rights, contact Ross Weiner, ICM Partners (rweiner@icmpartners.com)

POPCORN AT THE ODESSA © 2016 by Don Nigro. Reprinted by permission of Don Nigro. For performance rights, contact Samuel French, Inc., 212-206-8990, www.samuelfrench.com.

THE POWER OF DUFF© 2015 by Stephen Belber. Reprinted by permission of ICM Partners. For performance rights, contact Di Glazer, ICM Partners (dglazer@icmpartners.com)

PROMISING © 2016 by Michelle Elliott. Reprinted by permission of Susan Gurman, Susan Gurman Agency LLC. For performance rights, contact Susan Gurman (susan@gurmanagency.com)

PUDDING © 2009 by Michael Tooher. Reprinted by permission of Michael Tooher. For performance rights, contact Michael Tooher (michaeltooher@gmail.com)

THE SADTIC EP © 2016 by Graham Techler. Reprinted by permission of Graham Techler. For performance rights, contact Graham Techler (graham.techler@gmail.com)

SISTER SISTER © 2016 by Barbara Bluemthal-Ehrlich. Reprinted by permission of Barbara Blumenthal-Ehrlich. For performance rights, contact Barbara Blumenthal-Ehrlich (barbaretc@aol.com)

SIX BILLION ARCHITECTS © 2016 by Mark Andrew. Reprinted by permission of Mark Andrew. The entire text is published by Smith and Kraus in 2016: The Best 10-Minute Plays. For performance rights, contact Mark Andrew (mark@scenario.net.au)

STET © 2016 by Kim Davies. Reprinted by permission of ICM Partners. For performance rights, contact Di Glazer, ICM Partners (dglazer@icmpartners.com)

STONE COLD SOBER © 2016 by Macee Binns. Reprinted by permission of Macee Binns. For performance rights, contact Macee Binns (maceebinns@hotmail.com)

STUDENT BODY © 2016 by Frank Winters. Reprinted by permission of ICM Partners. For performance rights, contact Broadway Play Publishing, 212-772-8334, www.broadwayplaypubl.com

SUBTENANT © 2016 by Dan Hirsch. Reprinted by permission of Daniel Hirsch. For performance rights, contact Dan Hirsch (danieljayhirsch@gmail.com)

THE SURROGATE © 2016 by Patricia Cotter. Reprinted by permission of Susan Gurman, Susan Gurman Agency LLC. For performance rights, contact Susan Gurman (susan@gurmanagency.com)

TAKEN © 2016 by Susan Jackson. Reprinted by permission of Susan Jackson. For performance rights, contact Susan Jackson (susjcks5@aol.com)

THE TALENTED ONES © 2016 by Yussef El Guindi. Reprinted by permission of Leah Hamos, The Gersh Agency. For performance rights, contact Leah Hamos (lhamos@gershny.com)

THE TANGO © 2016 by Elayne Heilveil. Reprinted by permission of Elayne Heilveil. The entire text is published by Smith and Kraus in 2017: The Best 10-Minute Plays. For performance rights, contact Elayne Heilveil (elaynerh@aol.com)

THIS RANDOM WORLD © 2015 by Steven Dietz. Reprinted by permission of Beth Blickers, Agency for the Performing Arts. For performance rights, contact Beth Blickers (bblickers@apa-agency.com)

TOLSTOY IN NEW JERSEY © 2015 by Sam Bobrick. Reprinted by permission of Amy Wagner, Abrams Artists. For performance rights, contact Amy Wagner (amy.wagner@abramsartny.com)

TRANSit © 2016 by Darren Canady. Reprinted by permission of the author. For performance rights, contact Alexis Williams, Bret Adams Ltd. (awilliams@bretadamsltd.net)

VAUDEVILLE © 1997 by Laurence Carr. Reprinted by permission of Laurence Carr. For performance rights, contact Laurence Carr (carrlarry@optonline.net)

WARSONG © 2016 by Gregory Strasser. Reprinted by permission of Gregory Strasser. For performance rights, contact Gregory Strasser (gk.strasser@gmail.com)

WASTE LAND © 2016 by Don Nigro. Reprinted by permission of Don Nigro. For performance rights, contact Samuel French, Inc., 212-206-8990, www.samuelfrench.com

WHAT WE'LL DO © 2000 by Sheila Callaghan. Reprinted by permission of Chris Till, Creative Artists Agency. For performance rights, contact Chris Till (ctill@caa.com)

WEAPON OF MASS IMPACT, Part II (3) © 2016 by Brett Neveu. Reprinted by permission of Brett Neveu. For performance rights, contact Broadway Play Publishing, 212-772-8334, www.broadwayplaypubl.com

WHAT WE'RE UP AGAINST © 2016 by Theresa Rebeck. Reprinted by permission of Smith & Kraus, Inc. For performance rights, contact Samuel French, Inc., 212-206-8990, www.samuelfrench.com

WORLD BUILDERS © 2016 by Johnna Adams. Reprinted by permission of Alexis Williams, Bret Adams Ltd. For performance rights, contact Alexis Williams (awilliams@bretadamsltd.net)